W9-AOV-622

No Regrets

Three Discussions

EDITED BY DAYNA TORTORICI

Transcribed by Hanna Backman, Liza Batkin,
Laura Cremer, Noah Hurowitz, Elias Rodriques,
and Emily Wang

Π+1 RESEARCH BRANCH SMALL BOOKS SERIES #5

Π+1 FOUNDATION   NEW YORK

©2013 by n+1 Foundation, Inc. All rights reserved.

Published 2013 by n+1 Foundation

68 Jay Street, Ste. 405

Brooklyn, New York

www.nplusonemag.com

Special thanks to Carla Blumenkranz, Amy Ellingson,
Camille Gervais, Mark Greif, Chad Harbach, Kaitlin Phillips,
and Namara Smith. Extra special thanks to Moira Donegan
and Emma Janaskie for their production support; to
Keith Gessen for his editorial advice, encouragement, and
enthusiasm as a test reader; and to the participants for sharing
their weekend afternoons with n+1.

Cover by Dan O. Williams / texttile.net

ISBN 978-0-9890782-3-8

Printed by the Sheridan Press
Manufactured in the United States of America

CONTENTS

INTRODUCTION

An earlier book of conversations on this subject was called *What We Should Have Known*. It existed to give some guidance to college students—or roughly college-aged people—on what to read. The participants, all writers and editors close to *n+1* magazine, were asked: What books are worth reading? What did you read too late, or too soon? What changed your life?

The book turned out to be full of regrets. The speakers regretted their majors, what they read, what they didn't read. I read the book when I was still in college, and even I developed regrets after reading it. Here was an incredible list of books I'd never heard of, books I could have been reading instead of the ones I'd been assigned. I had already wasted two years reading the wrong things! This was the irony of the project. *What We Should Have Known* chronicled other people's regrets so that I might have none. And yet, as the book acknowledged, this made no sense. No sane young person is capable of learning without error or regret. The idea that anyone could become herself more quickly, or less painfully, by not making the necessary mistakes, was a perfectionist's fantasy. Maybe for this reason, the parts of the book I liked best were those that rejected regret out of hand. "Why should we regret anything?" Marco Roth asked in the second panel. "You make mistakes, you're supposed to be allowed to make mistakes. . . . Why did [Proust] spend so much time with the Guermantes? Why did he hang out with the anti-Dreyfusard snobs? In order to become Proust."

Since *n+1* published *What We Should Have Known* in 2007, the community surrounding it has expanded. Six years isn't a long time, but it is long enough for the cast of characters around a small magazine to change, and this seemed reason enough to repeat the experiment of *What We Should Have Known*. When the time came, I decided to include only women. I had several reasons, none of them entirely satisfying. One was that I already knew what the men in my life had read. The women, by contrast, were harder to shake down for lists of influences, and I suspected their lists would be different. Another was that the word *should* has a special place in the lives of women, as it's been a tool of their subjection through social strictures ("women should be X") and their emancipation through feminism ("women should reject the authority of anyone who says they should be X, or Y, or Z, or anything else"). *Should*, in other words, gives us both *The Rules* and the injunction to break them. I wanted to know how these pressures on women as women did or didn't intersect with their lives as readers, writers, artists, and thinkers; how the *should*s that stalk women through life influenced the *should* of what we should have known. Finally, I knew that women speak to one another differently in rooms without men. Not better, not more honestly, not more or less intelligently—just differently, and in a way one doesn't see portrayed as often as one might like.

The challenge posed by a book containing only women was well put by Susan Sontag (a figure surprisingly absent from the conversations that follow) in her introduction to Annie Leibovitz's monograph *Women*. "A book of photographs of women must, whether it intends to or not, raise the question of women—there is no equivalent 'question of men,'" she wrote. "Men, unlike women, are not a work in progress. . . . No book of photographs of men would be interrogated in the same way." Similarly, no book of conversations featuring only women will skate by without answering for itself in advance. That women are a "work in progress" means something different to this book than I think it did to Sontag, and perhaps more literal—*No Regrets* is, straightforwardly, a book of women talking about the processes of becoming themselves. But I take Sontag's point to heart. It might be unfortunate that these conversations make a statement even before they begin to speak. On the other hand, if they must make a statement—an argument for more casual depictions of smart, interesting women; a refusal to represent smart women in a way that marks them out as supposed "exceptions" to women universally; a call for more written records of conversations between women that capture everything that's unique to them, and everything that's not—those are statements I'm happy for us to make.

Dayna Tortorici
November 5, 2013

GROUP ONE

July 6, 2013

Kristin Dombek (Philadelphia, PA, 1972)
Sara Marcus (Washington, DC, 1977)
Dawn Lundy Martin (Hartford, CT, 1972)
Sarah Resnick (Kitchener-Waterloo, ON, Canada, 1980)
Moderator: **Dayna Tortorici** (Santa Monica, CA, 1989)

DAYNA TORTORICI: I want to open with a question that I admit is a slanted question. It's also a yes-or-no question, so it's easy. Do you have regrets? Do you think there are things you should have read, or did you think there were things you should've been reading, between the ages of 17 and 25, roughly?

(*A very long pause.*)

DAWN LUNDY MARTIN: Did we feel then, or do we feel now?

DAYNA TORTORICI: Both. Then and now. So, two yes-or-no questions.

SARAH RESNICK: There were things I would have liked to have read, although I don't know that I would characterize this feeling as regret. It's a word laden with all kinds of heavy emotions, like sadness and mourning . . . I don't want to think about my reading or not-reading in that way. I think that this sense of having missed something, even the sense of failure, is important to experience at a young age.

DAWN LUNDY MARTIN: I wouldn't use the word *regret*. A sense of an absence is what I generally felt at that age, that there were categories of texts that were missing from my instruction but I did not necessarily know what they were. I guess in retrospect those missing categories of texts affected the way I saw myself, because those were often queer texts, or African American texts, or feminist texts.

KRISTIN DOMBEK: I definitely felt a strong sense of *should* all the time, of what I should be reading, during that whole period. But when I look back, the thing I regret more is *how* I read, probably because of the *should*. I wish that I had read differently.

SARA MARCUS: I have a lot of trouble with the idea of regret, because if there's one thing I was falling short on in those years it was trusting my own instincts. And so the only things I regret not reading back then are the things I had a vague wish for but didn't know how to find.

Kerouac vs. Hemingway; Kristeva, Butler, Irigaray

DAYNA TORTORICI: On the subject of *should.* Can you describe when you first felt like you should be reading something, and why you thought you should be reading it?

I can give an example. When I was a teenager, I read with a sort of perverse determination to cure myself of two things. One was being from Los Angeles, and two was being a woman, because I didn't want to be either of those things. If I could pass as this other kind of person, I thought, I could go to college on the East Coast, and be a kind of, oh, I don't know . . .

KRISTIN DOMBEK: A man?

DAYNA TORTORICI: A man, yes. So I read things that were very "boy canon." I don't remember how exactly I knew to read them, there was definitely no one telling me to, at least not until later in high school. Though at some point Amazon started publishing these lists like, "So

You'd Like to . . . Read the Greatest Books of All Time?"
and I would consult those.

I read a lot of stuff, not only over my head—like
Anatomy of Criticism when I was 17, or *Hopscotch* when
I was 15—but stuff that was pretty directly aggres-
sive toward me as a reader. I will never forget reading
Bukowski's *Post Office* and feeling so horrible, the way
that the narrator describes the thickness of ugly wom-
en's legs. I think it was the first time I felt like a book
that I was trying to identify with rejected me. Though I
did absorb it, and of course it made me hate my body or
whatever.

I felt these were the books I should be reading,
because they would make me more like a boy and also
more like an East Coast intellectual. Not all of them
were bad. Most were very good!

SARA MARCUS: I remember putting *On the Road* down the
first time a woman was mentioned. I was just like: "Fuck.
You." I was probably 15 or 16. And over the coming years
I realized that it was this canonical work, so I tried to
return to it, but every time I was just like, "Fuck you."

DAYNA TORTORICI: I've never finished it!

SARA MARCUS: I read Marilyn French's *The Women's
Room* the summer I was 14, and it was like getting a
measles shot or something—from then on, if there was

something that was trying to make me feel bad about myself, I would put it way over *there*. And I don't regret that. I think that it's fine, when you're young, to just take in things that make you feel like you can *do* things, and leave the rest for later. For instance, I didn't read *Portnoy's Complaint* until after college. And I really liked it! But I don't regret not reading it earlier.

I've still never finished *On the Road*, though.

DAYNA TORTORICI: Have you guys finished *On the Road*?

DAWN LUNDY MARTIN: Yeah.

SARAH RESNICK: Yes.

KRISTIN DOMBEK: Yeah.

DAYNA TORTORICI: All three of you have finished *On the Road*.

KRISTIN DOMBEK: Yeah, and I loved it at the time. It's funny, I know I was doing that a lot, reading to be a man or like a man, to get into this world, but then there were books that I couldn't read. For some reason I couldn't read Hemingway. I would get so *angry*. I just couldn't read him. And years later, I read Hemingway and wished I could have read him earlier. Because I might have learned to write fucking short sentences, which would've been really good.

But I don't know why I couldn't read Hemingway and I could read Kerouac, or I couldn't read Henry Miller for a while, and then I was really glad to be able to read Henry Miller. Bukowski, I read *Post Office*—I couldn't read him for a while—but I read it a few years ago and loved it. These things are mysterious to me.

SARAH RESNICK: I pretty much had a parallel experience of being able to read Kerouac but not Hemingway. I don't really know why. I was influenced by my older brother, and would read things he read—though he also really liked Hemingway, so that's not the reason.

I found Kerouac really exciting at that time. I was 14 or 15 when I read *On the Road*, and it was my first experience with a kind of break from conventions of "good writing." I'm not sure that I was so attuned yet to some of the criticisms that Sara suggested, of the female characters.

DAWN LUNDY MARTIN: I didn't have trouble reading mas-culinist texts like Hemingway. I kind of thought I was a boy anyway, for a long time, so I was just identifying. The parallel moment for me was reading texts that had prob-lematic moments around race, and being in a class—I went to school with all white kids—reading Faulkner, or Twain . . . and there were racialized moments that were really unconsidered, and a kind of discomfort around those moments. I felt real resistance, even to something like *To Kill a Mockingbird*. I wanted it to get considered in a different way. But I also felt like it couldn't just be me having this moment, around them, of feeling just *hot*. I didn't even know what the feeling was. Embarrassment? Shame?

And then kind of by happenstance, a friend's mother—I had only read maybe one other book by a black writer by the time I was 17—a friend's mother gave me *The Color Purple*. Which was fraught in all kinds of racial and gendered ways, but it felt like such a relief, that kind of honesty around these identities that were complicated in the other texts but that you couldn't talk about.

KRISTIN DOMBEK: So you didn't speak in class?

DAWN LUNDY MARTIN: No, it was impossible. I didn't have the language for it in that context. No one was providing us with a language. The only language would have been a language of resistance. But I didn't have the kind of analytical language with which to help others in the class, because, you know, the instructors weren't doing it.

DAYNA TORTORICI: Did you feel like you should be reading those books anyway and enjoying them?

DAWN LUNDY MARTIN: Absolutely! I mean they're great books, right? I kind of understood that there was a failure on the part of another person, but it felt like an internal failure as well. "Why can't I enjoy these books in the way that they should be enjoyed?"

KRISTIN DOMBEK: I was one of the people who "went French" in college, instead of German,* and one of the reasons was that I thought I was stupid, because I felt like language didn't work for me the way it did for—I was a philosophy major—Aristotle, for Kant. I experienced so many texts as violent in some way that just didn't make any sense. I thought I was dumb. Or that I didn't belong, because I had been homeschooled and I was Christian. And then when I read Kristeva and Derrida and Foucault, I was like, "Oh . . . other people think language is slippery!" So then that became the new religion.

SARAH RESNICK: I felt really ill-equipped when I first encountered the poststructuralists you just mentioned, like Irigaray and Kristeva and Butler. I wonder whether I would have experienced them differently if I'd had any background at all in history, or in philosophy, anything

---

* "Benjamin Kunkel: When I was in college there was a kind of either-or fatal choice that had to be made, at least for the type of people I knew. . . . It was either the Frankfurt School or poststructuralism. . . . There were the people who went French, and the people who went German." *What We Should Have Known*, 29–30.

that would have provided context. I ended up majoring in cultural studies after meandering in and out of other departments—I'd been taking classes in biology and calculus and environmental sciences—and the courses I took provided little, if any, social context beyond a vague sense of what these writers were reacting against. Of course that was sort of the point, that everything is a text, but some of my professors treated this stuff as gospel, as a kind of end point on the timeline of intellectual history. Nothing else mattered.

That shift from the very material orientation of science to the abstraction of theory was disorienting. Some of those texts could be inscrutable on first read. I knew I wasn't really getting it. And of course, because these writers were responding to one another, there's the issue of chronology: Who do you read first? Irigaray is talking about Marx, so if you haven't read Marx, then maybe you don't really understand what she's talking about. And if you're looking at Butler, she's responding to Kristeva and Irigaray. I was wildly underprepared—the experience of reading these texts was the experience of realizing that I didn't know much. I'm kind of glad that I encountered them in that way though, as a tangled mess that I had to work my way out of.

SARA MARCUS: I remember being a first-year in college and reading "Imitation and Gender Insubordination" and having everything crack open for me. I first began to identify as a queer feminist in the early and mid-'90s, and I felt like all of my intellectual and political activities and self-regard were obligated to line up in certain very literal ways—which Butler just *axed* in that essay. I read the line about, "I'm willing to appear as a lesbian on political occasions, but I would like to have it permanently unclear precisely what that signifies," and I was like, "Oh, wow! Amazing!" I realized that I could speak and act politically without being hemmed in by all the rigid ways that identity was being used then.

I went home and tried to read this essay to my mom. She's really into pop music, so I read her the part about Aretha Franklin—where Butler is like, "When Aretha Franklin sings, 'You make me feel *like* a natural woman,' that's pointing out that it's already a mimetic imitation of it, and what if Aretha were singing to me?" And I was like, "Mom, *get it?*" And she was like, blink blink.

DAYNA TORTORICI: Was it a gateway drug?

SARA MARCUS: Well, interestingly, what Sarah described started to happen. I was like, Well, I haven't read Hegel, and Hegel's really hard. So I actually didn't follow it up by reading a ton more Butler right away, but that "Imitation" essay had a profound influence on how I carried myself as a human being in the world. "Imitation and Gender Insubordination" is such an amazing essay because it's not super referential; it's really rooted in her experience and the limits of what you can derive from that. I don't believe there's a single Hegel footnote.

Angela Davis's library; Protests; Peers

SARA MARCUS: There was a point in my mid- or late twenties where I had this paroxysm of like, "Oh, 18-year-old Sara, why were you so rigid? Why did you have to read women? Why couldn't you be more expansive?" I just, whatever, I own it now. That's what I needed at 18. It's fine.

DAYNA TORTORICI: When was this?

SARA MARCUS: I guess around when I was getting an MFA. It was this period, which turned out to be a passing one, in which I resented my need for particularist identifications. Why couldn't I just be this general, vast brain?

Have any of the rest of you had . . . It sounds like you all were less resistant in youth than I was.

KRISTIN DOMBEK: No, I was really oppositional and resistant to all kinds of texts.

SARA MARCUS: Yeah?

KRISTIN DOMBEK: I would just throw them away. I feel ashamed of it, I don't know if I regret it. My students now are much better—they're much more mature than I was. They can read something they disagree with and not just push it away in the way that I did.

SARAH RESNICK: What did you throw away?

KRISTIN DOMBEK: Well, Hemingway, for example. But then—I read Marx and I was like, *No*. And then the next year I'd be like, "I'm a Marxist." I was a very conservative Christian coming into college. I was reading in the fundamentalist ways that I was trained in, and fighting them and trying to destroy them at the same time. When I went to college, professors started telling me to read the Bible differently. That was a big problem.

DAYNA TORTORICI: As literature?

KRISTIN DOMBEK: As authored in more complicated ways than, like, direct inspiration. I went to a Christian college, but there were liberal theologians who were saying this there. I had my first Bible class, and the professor said that the first five books weren't written by Moses. They were pulled together from J, P, and Q or whatever the sources are. And I flipped out completely.

My dad and a conservative theologian friend of his were sending me letters about how to deal with the brainwashing that they said was going to happen at a liberal college, and I wrote a paper that was basically against the class. I said, I can't write as if the Bible's not written by God directly via Moses. And then I went to the professor's office. And she sort of said, "You have to. This is the scholarly consensus. There's no doubt that the first five books of the Bible were written by J and P and Q and whoever." And so I left that school.

DAYNA TORTORICI: But you didn't ignore it.

KRISTIN DOMBEK: I didn't ignore it, but it took a while to get over that way of reading, either it's true or it's not true. Either it's true or it's evil. Either it's true or it's trying to hurt me. That way of reading stuck with me for a long time, even as I became an atheist and, you know, a liberal or whatever.

So I wonder about this reading to identify. It's totally necessary—we need what William James calls "an idea we can ride," at any given time—and then also it can really limit you.

DAWN LUNDY MARTIN: In certain situations it requires a kind of rigor to read the things that you identify with. The canon is always knocking really loudly at the door. When I was in college, I was reading out of anger. I was like, "These *fuckers*, they totally fucked my mind." Making me think that there was only a certain set of texts—a very small, narrow set of texts—that reflected this idea of identity. Later in life, after college, I met Angela Davis in Oakland and I became her dog-sitter, through a random set of happenings. I started reading through her bookshelves . . .

DAYNA TORTORICI: Her personal library?

DAWN LUNDY MARTIN: Her personal library. And then also reading through her life, her associations, watching her video library. Reading not only her autobiography but Assata Shakur's autobiography, and rereading *Malcolm X*. It felt important to a particular history, and also to my own political trajectory. I was just doing it, I wasn't talking about it with anyone. I was in grad school at the time, and on the grad school side I was reading Mallarmé in an experimental poetics program, and then, in secret, reading these sometimes badly written books. But it felt really important. Enduring that balance felt really rigorous.

KRISTIN DOMBEK: Weren't you also Gloria Steinem's house sitter or something?

DAWN LUNDY MARTIN: No, I was just hanging out at Gloria Steinem's house. Gloria was a big supporter and friend of the Third Wave Foundation, a young feminist organization I cofounded. I didn't house-sit. I sat with her.

SARAH RESNICK: I went to school in Montreal, and my second year, during final exams, I ended up in Quebec City to protest a summit for the proposed Free Trade Area of the Americas. It was a kind of NAFTA-plus-plus, now defunct, that would have extended the treaty's model of economic liberalization to all countries in the Americas except Cuba. Of course all the negotiations were going on in secret. This was the third summit on the agreement. The police had prepared for the weekend by erecting a two-and-a-half-mile long "security fence" around the meeting area, and dividing the downtown area into zones of risk.

I took a student-chartered bus to Quebec City with two friends. We didn't have any plans, we weren't part of any group, we were just showing up. Needless to say, we were really naive and unprepared. Over the course of the weekend, there were around fifty thousand protesters and something like six thousand police officers. There was a *lot* of tear gas—it was pervasive. I didn't have much in the way of protection aside from a bandana and some apple cider vinegar to soak it in—which, for the record, doesn't help much. By day two, the gas was impossible to escape no matter what zone you were in. The police would do this thing where they approached in formation, marching in step, banging their batons on their knees in unison. I now recognize this as a deliberate intimidation tactic. It worked!

This was my first experience with any kind of state-sanctioned repression or violence. I was terrified. I didn't know what to do with myself—where to go, where to stand, who to talk to. And it felt like wherever I did end up it was because I had run away from something else—the police, a tear-gas canister. I stuck it out, though. Part of the trouble was that I had so little analysis to bring to the situation. I understood why I was there, why all these people were there, but I didn't really have the tools to make sense of the larger movement. I'd seen the "Battle of Seattle" on television a few years earlier. But I knew next to nothing about the larger global justice movement.

DAYNA TORTORICI: So what did you do?

SARAH RESNICK: What did I do?

DAYNA TORTORICI: Who did you look to for cues about how to find the answers to those questions?

SARAH RESNICK: I looked to friends, mostly, though I think my friends were equally at sea. I read what I could—the newspaper, magazines, analysis. I really should give credit to Naomi Klein's *No Logo*, published a year and a half earlier, even though it's not a book I would necessarily recommend now. Many of its insights would feel commonplace, but back then she put words to an experience that was very familiar but not well understood: products themselves no longer mattered, what corporations cared about was marketing and brand identity. We were all being sold a lifestyle. And by connecting all this to the outsourcing of manufacturing labor overseas and the influx of service-sector work in North America, she pulled together a lot of big ideas in a very accessible way.

DAYNA TORTORICI: Did you have peers, people you were reading with at certain points in your life, who were important to you? Or has reading always felt like a solitary pursuit? I guess having somebody else's library is sort of like having a peer—another person's mind guiding you.

KRISTIN DOMBEK: Growing up, to me, as a reader, is starting to read with people. Reading groups. The thing that you described, Sarah, really resonates with me—experiencing a moment where you're like, this is history. This is what's happening. I can feel history and I can't understand it, and I can't understand how to influence and be a part of it. And I need to find people who are trying to understand it, too, and who will help me find the books that will help. For me there were a few big events like that. One was when this guy, David Noeble, brought *The Gay Agenda* to my college in the mid-'90s. Pat Robertson funded it, and it was this documentary that was sent around to congressmen, a video . . .

SARA MARCUS: Oh, it was a video of Gay Pride parades!

DAWN LUNDY MARTIN: Like propaganda.

KRISTIN DOMBEK: Yes, propaganda. It was a "documentary" about the prevalence of golden showers and fisting among the gay population. It was shots of the Pride Parade in San Francisco and New York with this ominous music underneath—*dun, dun, dun*—and it showed at my school. And there was this mass hate festival. This was when I was still sort of a Christian, and I thought, "This is not OK." These were supposed to be my people, you know? Christians, watching this. And that made me find people who would tell me what to read, to understand a whole bunch of things.

I found this group of people at my school who were trying to fight for gay and lesbian rights, and trying to change some of the administrative policies at the school, and I started reading what I saw they were reading. I think that's when I started reading Judith Butler.

DAYNA TORTORICI: Do you remember the first Butler that you read?

KRISTIN DOMBEK: *Gender Trouble*?

DAYNA TORTORICI: What's the first Butler everyone read?

DAWN LUNDY MARTIN: *Gender Trouble.*

SARAH RESNICK: *Gender Trouble.*

"It had been like dying"; Grace Paley

DAYNA TORTORICI: What books made you want to write? What writers redefined ways of writing for you, ways of thinking?

DAWN LUNDY MARTIN: I mentioned Mallarmé earlier. One of the things was Mallarmé's "A Tomb for Anatole," which was published after his death. His son dies when he's 6, I think, and Mallarmé attempts to write about this loss. He attempts to write these poems and he just keeps writing and stopping, it's very broken. He never finishes the book. I kind of understood, in that incarnation, the power of failure, and how to speak about absence or loss.

Then later on, a poet I returned to again and again was Myung Mi Kim. She's a Korean American poet who especially in her early work struggles through the possibility that the self might exist in between national identities. She immigrated to the United States from Korea when she was 9, and at some moment she lost her ability to speak Korean, but she also couldn't speak

English quite yet. So in her writing, later, she's struggling through this moment of being both inside and apart from both nation and language. What does that produce?

KRISTIN DOMBEK: I write, you know, essays, and the first real essays that made me want to write in college were Annie Dillard's essays, and so I tried to write like Annie Dillard for a long time, which is really bad.

DAYNA TORTORICI: You're wincing. Why are you wincing?

KRISTIN DOMBEK: I'm embarrassed about it—I hadn't really read any other essays, so I think it was . . . She's so over the top, right? She'll begin an essay—like "Total Eclipse," she'll begin with, "*It had been like dying.*" It had been like dying! She's talking about driving down a mountain to watch an eclipse, and she's like, "It had been like dying."

SARAH RESNICK: "A weasel is wild."

KRISTIN DOMBEK: "A weasel is wild," yes. All these moments of intense drama in just a walk through the woods or whatever. I really imitated her for a while . . . but she made me want to write. And David Foster Wallace is the most contagious writer I know. You read him and then you find yourself writing like him and you try to stop. But I wish I had read Didion a little bit more in college to balance the Dillard. I assign her now and I see my students resist, they want to get all the emotion they can into their sentences . . . and—I don't know, maybe they shouldn't try to write like Didion yet. But I wish I had started sooner.

SARA MARCUS: I didn't find the cleanness of Didion useful until much later. At that age I was obsessed with the '30s—I did my senior essay on reportage in the American communist magazine *New Masses*—and these were the people who made me want to write. It was very gorgeous writing and very, very political. I needed to see that you could write without abandoning the fight. That was *the* number one thing for me. And I got that from Meridel Le Sueur. I got it from Erskine Caldwell.

The summer I moved to New York I found a book of Grace Paley's short stories on top of a garbage can on East 9th Street. People had been telling me to read her, and I had been resisting—stories about mothers or middle-aged married couples or old divorced couples didn't feel important to me. But I picked it up, and it's a woman and her husband having an argument, and it's like, "And then when we were at the protest meeting that other week you were flirting with that woman. . . ." I just thought, This is it. Here it is! You have your relationships and you have your political commitments and in this incredibly marvelous condensed language, and it's not hackneyed or forced.

SARAH RESNICK: I love her stories. And I continue to be impressed by her ability to remain a committed activist even as she saw success as a writer. One never subsumed the other. To live that kind of dual commitment—and to be good at both—that's hard. Another writer I thought of as we were talking is Adrian Nicole LeBlanc.

DAYNA TORTORICI: Who?

SARAH RESNICK: *Random Family*, Adrian Nicole LeBlanc. She was a journalist at the *Voice* in the late '80s, where she covered the trial of Boy George, this drug dealer from the South Bronx who built a small empire around his own brand of heroin. During the trial reporting she met his girlfriend and the girlfriend of the girlfriend's younger brother, and she shadowed these two women and their expanding families for the next eleven years. Eleven years! That's a really long time. It's an amazing, amazing work of reportage. And never once does she try to explain anyone's actions. She doesn't try to justify or even to defend them. It's a really heroic work.

Old passions; *Natural Born Killers*

DAYNA TORTORICI: What about books that mattered to you at a certain time that don't anymore? Books that you don't revisit?

DAWN LUNDY MARTIN: This is embarrassing, but I would say something like *Stone Butch Blues* by Leslie Feinberg, or *Zami* by Audre Lorde. I've tried to revisit them, and there are moments where I'm just like—*eckh*. You just want both of those books to have a better editor. In both of those cases, when I was reading them, I was really overwhelmed by the content of the stories. I remember having this really visceral emotional response to them. Crying while reading *Stone Butch Blues*. Jerking off while reading *Zami*. I can't imagine that now. I just get so caught up in the—the prose moments that I don't appreciate, let's say. And the only reason that I read them later is because I decided to teach them in a class.

KRISTIN DOMBEK: It's funny, in some ways the most revelatory text becomes the one that you're most ashamed of. I didn't find any sort of feminist text to change my life in college. Adrienne Rich, maybe. But the big moment for me in college was seeing (*quietly*) . . . *Natural Born Killers.*

EVERYONE: What?

DAYNA TORTORICI: Say it again!

KRISTIN DOMBEK: *Natural Born Killers*? I was such a total pacifist and I would walk out of any movie where there was violence against women. I would put down any book that felt like that. I was such a *pacifist*, I wouldn't kill the mice in my house, and then they'd overrun my house.

And then—why am I telling you this story? This is really embarrassing. But, for some reason, *Natural Born Killers* I could watch, and I know now why. In the opening scene, Juliette Lewis gets mad at this guy for flirting with her when she's just dancing by herself playing the jukebox. And she kills him, with her bare hands. She's like, "Are you flirting with me?" and she kills him. That's the opening scene. And I could watch that whole movie. It was distanced enough, and also there was this female character killing people. Very simple. It feels dumb now, but it changed my life. I then made this sort of study of male violence. That's when I read everything that Cormac McCarthy ever wrote—

DAYNA TORTORICI: Whoa.

KRISTIN DOMBEK: —and sort of made this study.

DAYNA TORTORICI: In a row?

KRISTIN DOMBEK: Well, after college, I spent a bunch of years. Somehow studying male-on-male violence and male-on-female violence was really important to me for a long time. To face it. To look at it and to recognize my own violence and anger. I'd watch every big action movie as if it were really important for me to understand. I have no interest in that stuff now. Cormac McCarthy or action movies.

Get off that tambourine and stop texting

DAYNA TORTORICI: What writers inspired completism—made you want to read their whole body of work?

DAWN LUNDY MARTIN: The first writer who inspired me to read everything was Anne Sexton. I said this to you yesterday, Kristin, how I was really interested in how she fetishizes suffering . . .

KRISTIN DOMBEK: Oh, that's who you were talking about! I thought you were talking about me.

DAWN LUNDY MARTIN: Anne Sexton and Kristin Dombek!

KRISTIN DOMBEK: Because I've been thinking about fetishizing suffering, and so I thought, "I know how to do that." But you were talking about Anne Sexton.

DAWN LUNDY MARTIN: I remember reading all of her books of poems and then reading all of her letters. It was when I was just also learning to become a poet and was thinking about the composition of the metaphor. There's this obsessive quality of her work, leaning into this particular space over the course of her short life, and she's able to work there without letting it go. That's something I think I've learned from her, how to attend to this thing that's compelling you to write it over and over and over again and for it to be consistently fresh. But also I was interested in the life around that, which is when I got to the letters. I was obsessed with her self-indulgence, what the canon later names "confessional poetry." Even when she rewrote the Grimms' fairy tales in *Transformations* it was all about her. I had a kind of as yet untapped prelinguistic knowing that I, too, would mine my life in some art form. Sexton was the first person who introduced me to that possibility. That she was a deeply problematic figure who struggled with depression and mania and committed suicide at the age of 46 made her even more compelling to me.

DAYNA TORTORICI: What about things that weren't books that changed your life?

SARA MARCUS: In the immediate post-college time, free improvisation was more important to me than books— going to Tonic to see eight people get on stage and play.

There was a lot less heaviness attached; you were never going to have heard the same night at Tonic as somebody else. "Did you see David S. Ware at the Knitting Factory on August 8th?" No, I was busy. It's not the same as, "Did you read whatever book?"

And punk rock, but that was a little earlier. I think punk rock bleeds into free improv in a way. And The Ex! Seeing The Ex at the apex of free improv and punk rock.

DAYNA TORTORICI: What's The Ex?

SARA MARCUS: Oh! They're this amazing Dutch punk band . . .

SARAH RESNICK: They're amazing.

SARA MARCUS: I feel like there was a time when every six months I was heading down to Leonard Street to see The Ex at the Knit.

SARAH RESNICK: My second year at McGill, I didn't go back home in the summer, I stayed in Montreal, and I became friends with a lot of people who were not in college. Some of them were older, some of them weren't. I didn't really think much of it at the time, but no one had gone to university. And yet they were all extremely intelligent people who were doing a lot of really interesting things. Writers, musicians. This is embarrassing, but I used to go to . . . after-hours, kind of rave stuff, a lot at that time. That's something I don't ever need to revisit, but it was—it was kind of really meaningful. It expanded my world, which for various reasons had been pretty narrow until that point. I, too, was raised in a really religious family, and there seemed to be this one path that you went down: be a good student and that's your way out of this. So that was really eye-opening to me, that not everyone had felt the need to do this. I felt buoyed by the example of my non-college-going friends, and considered taking time off, or leaving. Those options didn't feel entirely right either, so I stuck it out, and took a reduced course load. In retrospect, I'm glad that I did.

DAWN LUNDY MARTIN: For nonbooks, the first person who came to my mind was Adrian Piper, who's a performance artist. She did some installation work, some painting. She identifies as a black woman but sometimes can be physically unrecognizable as black, and at other times she's really recognizable as black. It just depends on the context. And that's part of the impetus for her. She has these two self-portraits that she's painted; one is "Self-Portrait Exaggerating My Negroid Features," and the other is "Self-Portrait as a Nice White Lady," I think is the title. And from the latter woman's mouth there's this bubble that says, "Whut choo lookin at mofo."

KRISTIN DOMBEK: I feel like the thing that I spent most of my time doing in college when I wasn't studying or reading was watching guys play music.

DAYNA TORTORICI: Guys you knew?

KRISTIN DOMBEK: Yeah.

DAYNA TORTORICI: I did a lot of that too.

KRISTIN DOMBEK: Just sitting around in living rooms . . .

DAYNA TORTORICI: "Jam sessions."

KRISTIN DOMBEK: Sitting through jam sessions.

DAYNA TORTORICI: Yes.

KRISTIN DOMBEK: I often find myself in this warehouse in Bushwick where people circle through and just play, for hours and hours. There are these 18-year-old boys who seem to almost live there and are really dominating, and then there are these girls who are sitting there—now they're texting—but they're just listening to the boys play music, for hours and hours and hours. And I keep watching, you know, and I just . . .

DAWN LUNDY MARTIN: Sara, your face.

SARA MARCUS: What's my face?

DAWN LUNDY MARTIN: Not a happy one.

SARA MARCUS: It hurts! I'm sorry, it really hurts.

KRISTIN DOMBEK: They play the tambourine, you know? And they sit. I've been thinking about how much time I spent doing that.

DAYNA TORTORICI: How much time *did* you spend doing that?

KRISTIN DOMBEK: A lot of time! And I recently started playing bass, and so I'm not just sitting and listening anymore. But after so many years of not . . . I was thinking about these girls, because I keep wanting to shake them and just say, "It doesn't matter if you fuck it up, if you fuck it up because you don't know the chord changes. It doesn't matter." You know? Get off that tambourine. I mean, seriously. (*Pause.*) And stop texting!

____

Memorable pairings; Eileen Myles; Lynne Tillman; Native Agents

DAYNA TORTORICI: OK, lightning fill-in-the-blank. Any final thoughts, or things that changed your life?

DAWN LUNDY MARTIN: I had a transformative moment once rereading Judith Butler and the *Story of O* simultaneously.

KRISTIN DOMBEK: Which Judith Butler?

DAWN LUNDY MARTIN: *Gender Trouble.*

EVERYONE: *Gender Trouble*!!

DAYNA TORTORICI: Maybe that's a better question. Memorable pairings?

KRISTIN DOMBEK: I have a few, but a book I wish I'd read earlier is *Black Reconstruction in America*. I read it in grad school and really wished I'd read it in college. I was reading that around the same time I was reading *Invisible Man*. *Black Reconstruction* not only changed the story about race in American history for me, but challenged my habits of thinking. I had not really read much sociology or history before grad school, because I was all Frenchy and humanities and stuff, and so I wasn't asking the question of how you can figure out what large groups of people are doing and how change happens over time. The question of what kind of evidence you need, what kind of methods you need. But people do this, amazingly. Try to answer these questions. Beautifully, brilliantly in DuBois's case. And I didn't know. I wish I knew that as an undergrad.

SARAH RESNICK: I maybe wish I had read some of the Marxist feminists earlier.

DAYNA TORTORICI: Any in particular?

SARAH RESNICK: Mariarosa Dalla Costa and Selma James's "The Power of Women and the Subversion of the Community," a great essay. Silvia Federici's collection of essays, *Revolution at Point Zero*. Also, Johanna Brenner and Maria Ramas's "Rethinking Women's Oppression" in the *New Left Review*. All of these provide a solid introduction to the idea of social reproduction; that there's all kinds of work—mental, physical, and emotional—required to maintain and reproduce our economy. I see the limits of these texts and the reasons they were rejected by cultural feminists, but the question is how to move forward from there now. Writers like Kathi Weeks are making an effort, and her book *The Problem with Work* is worth reading for all kinds of reasons.

KRISTIN DOMBEK: The academic work I think everyone should read, more recently, is all the stuff about post-humanism, the work across disciplines trying to get humans out of the center of our ways of thinking about ethics, about animals, about ecology. Cary Wolfe, Donna Haraway to some extent, Derrida before he died. I feel like it's the most important . . . trend. I don't think we can understand economic inequality among humans, or why people don't care about the environment, or how to stop violence even within our species, without under-standing the ways in which we've organized human cultures around dominating other animals, and trying to distinguish ourselves from them.

DAYNA TORTORICI: Where would you tell someone to start on that subject?

KRISTIN DOMBEK: With Cary Wolfe's anthology, *Zoon-tologies*, which has a bunch of essays from different dis-ciplines, and some journalism. It also has Derrida's "The Animal That Therefore I Am" essay, and Cary Wolfe makes the argument for why it's important to think with animals. And then Coetzee's *The Lives of Animals*.

SARA MARCUS: I wish I had read Lynne Tillman and Eileen Myles earlier. I think my life might have been different if I had read *Chelsea Girls* when I was 20 and known it was the book I was looking for. I was diligently trying to find some brilliantly written prose that didn't respect boundaries between fiction and nonfiction and that dealt with young queer women hanging around in cities and fucking up. People would suggest that I go read Sarah Waters, which wasn't what I wanted at all. And weirdly, I'd actually heard Eileen Myles read poetry on this feminist punk compilation, *Move Into the Villa Villakula*, but I didn't realize that she had published books of poetry, and I certainly didn't know about *Chelsea Girls*. Pre-internet generation! If it hadn't been out then, I could get over it. But it was published when I was in eleventh grade. So I'm angry! Why didn't anybody tell me about it then? Same with Lynne Tillman. It turns out I really needed to read Lynne Tillman in college, but I didn't even know she existed.

SARAH RESNICK: I would say the same thing. Was the Semiotext(e) Native Agents series important for anyone during that time?

SARA MARCUS: I didn't know about it! I had no idea!

SARAH RESNICK: I had no idea it existed either.

———

Reasons to read at all

SARA MARCUS: Much of what we're talking about is a consumption of culture . . . We're not talking quite directly about creating culture. It's interesting that we're talking about what we consume as being implicitly relevant because of what we make out of it, but that's been just outside the circle of our conversation.

KRISTIN DOMBEK: I think there's something to be said for stopping consuming altogether, including reading, for a while. I recently didn't read for a couple years and didn't watch television, didn't watch very many movies. I read, like, five books.

SARA MARCUS: Because you were at work on something else?

KRISTIN DOMBEK: I was at work on all kinds of things. I was becoming part of a community of people who were making things. I didn't think about it, it wasn't a plan. I just had a big life change and sort of dropped out, and then became the most productive, at writing, and sort of the happiest I've ever been. It's not a recommendation, but there is something about this, the position of consuming vs. the position of figuring out how to fill the world around you with art and action, which you can only do with people.

There's this moment in *Super Sad True Love Story* where the protagonist has a bookshelf and a young girlfriend he brings home, and she sees his books and she's like, "Ew! They *smell!*" It's a bit in the future, and no one has books on their bookshelves anymore. That scares me, but I had that kind of abject experience with my books recently. At the end of the first year of not really reading, my books had been in storage, and I unpacked them, and I was like, *Why?* I'd paid to keep these in storage for a year while I lived book-free and then I pulled them all out, and it was the opposite of the Benjamin essay. I was unpacking my library and feeling horrified. I saw that the reason I kept so many of the books was because they said something about me, like, "I read them, I got a PhD, I made it through all this, I read Hegel, I have Hegel." And I was repulsed by my past need to identify, my attachment to them as objects, as things that I collected.

So I guess I would say to a younger person: the reason to read is to find new ways of thinking, new ways of seeing the world, new ways of writing that are useful, and that are useful in conversation with people around you. To make things more just and more pleasurable. It doesn't matter, in the end, the right things or the wrong things, or how smart you are.

DAWN LUNDY MARTIN: Well . . . it doesn't matter to you, anymore. "I clearly am smart."

KRISTIN DOMBEK: I just wish I had read a little less for identification.

DAYNA TORTORICI: But who knows who's going to walk your dog and read your library? Maybe those books are not just for you. +

GROUP TWO

July 21, 2013

Carla Blumenkranz (Miami, FL, 1983)
Emily Gould (Washington, DC, 1981)
Emily Witt (Allentown, PA, 1981)

DAYNA TORTORICI: Welcome to the second round of *No Regrets*. To start: do you regret what you chose to read in college?

EMILY GOULD: A few years ago I would've said, unequivocally, yes. But now I am starting to see a pattern that I didn't before. I feel, in a very hippie-dippy way, that things have come to me at the right time. But who knows? In general I try not to have regrets.

CARLA BLUMENKRANZ: I still feel so engaged in the narrative of my reading and the kind of person it's made me that it would feel almost life-denying to say that I regret it. I read a lot of experimental literature when I was in my early twenties that was directed by professors and may or may not have been relevant or even good for me. But I don't know that I regret it, exactly.

DAYNA TORTORICI: If you were to go back in time and intercept your 18-to-22-year-old self, and say, "I know what you think you're doing, but you should just read *this* book, *this* author," who or what would it be? Or to what would you say, "No, no, no, trust me, don't do that"?

EMILY WITT: Are we talking about college?

DAYNA TORTORICI: College, being a college-aged person.

EMILY WITT: I would tell myself not to take classes with a pop-culture component. I wasn't an English major and I didn't take very many English classes, but in the one or two that I did we read A. S. Byatt and Bret Easton Ellis—stuff you can read on your own. You understand the world of those books, you live in it. But Henry James or Faulkner, it's different. I think college should be a time for reading difficult books that are not easily accessible to you.

EMILY GOULD: At that age you still have the ability to grapple with things that are difficult, which does go away when you get older. You lose those big chunks of unstructured time that some of us were lucky enough to have then. If you try to read *Middlemarch* for the first time in your mid-twenties, you may not be able to read it the way you would have if it had been assigned to you. Just, for example—not that anyone ever tried to bring *Middlemarch* on a really disastrous vacation with her then boyfriend's family, and despite being trapped in a tiny ski cottage during some terrible snowstorms, so no one was skiing, and it only had one bathroom, and there were seven people, there was no TV . . .

DAYNA TORTORICI: Sounds like a good time to read *Middlemarch*.

EMILY GOULD: And I still read *The Time Traveler's Wife* instead of *Middlemarch*! For whatever reason, I couldn't do it. Maybe dumbness.

CARLA BLUMENKRANZ: I read so many novels in college. I took almost all English classes and creative writing classes and history classes. I don't regret any of the things I read, but I regret the way that I approached them. I had this idea that I was training myself to be some kind of artist, and I had naive ideas about what that meant. I tried to be very intense and ascetic about how I thought about reading and writing, and I really tried to make my life difficult. I would tell myself to stop . . . doing that.

DAYNA TORTORICI: To stop pursuing difficulty?

CARLA BLUMENKRANZ: To stop approaching literature in my life and my life through literature in an inhumane way.

EMILY GOULD: I would give the exact opposite advice to my young self, because I was the exact opposite person. I pretty much only read for pleasure, entertainment, painkilling, distraction. The only times I read in the way you described were when I wanted to impress my really impressive friend Normandy. She's the reason I read *Carrie* by Stephen King when I was in sixth grade, and she's the reason I read Judith Butler. Everything that was a little bit beyond what I would naturally have been attracted to I read because I wanted her to think I was smart. To this day I read things so that I'll have something to talk to her about. I would tell my young self to read things that are hard for me for reasons other than trying to impress Normandy.

DAYNA TORTORICI: Do you think difficulty is a subjective experience? Is the experience of reading so-called difficult texts in college different for men and women based on what counts as a "difficult text" there?

CARLA BLUMENKRANZ: I know people feel differently, but I find the idea that men and women fundamentally read differently really depressing. Maybe it's because I grew up feeling gender-neutral as a reader. Instinctively I think, no, it's not any different, because that was my experience. But it's interesting to me when people raise that, because if all along I was making some kind of gender error of identification, or if there were ways these things were secretly barred to me that I didn't know about, that would be quite disturbing.

EMILY WITT: I said that I regretted taking kind of bullshit classes. When I started reading theory, both in college and out of college—Foucault, Roland Barthes, all that stuff—it was so exciting to me. It changed the way that I thought about and perceived the world, and the fact that it was difficult to read, that the style could be thorny, added to that.

Outside of college, reading *Infinite Jest* for the first time, between my junior and my senior year, was a formative experience. It's not that I thought I was dumb, but I thought that reading didn't have the same power to captivate me as it did when I was young. I was reading books that were sort of mediocre for three or four years, and then I realized, "No, I can have that narcotic feeling of reading a book that changes the way I think about the world." A lot of that to me was related to size and depth and complexity. Then I thought, "Why? Why was I reading some stupid book by Thomas Friedman in this class?"

DAYNA TORTORICI: What was your major?

EMILY WITT: Art Semiotics and Portuguese and Brazilian Studies.

DAYNA TORTORICI: So did you encounter theory stuff in Semiotics, or were you more Art than Semiotics?

EMILY WITT: I was more theory. Unlike a lot of people, I didn't know about any of that stuff when I came to college. If you had said "Foucault" to me I wouldn't have known what you were talking about. I got into it with a film studies class. It started with the Lumière brothers, Eisenstein, *Birth of a Nation*, all the way to less familiar films like the work of the Ethiopian director Haile Gerima and Michael Snow's *Wavelength*. All that changed the way that I watched films. I couldn't believe it, almost, to read something like Laura Mulvey's psychoanalytic analysis of narrative cinema, where she talks about "woman as image, man as bearer of the look," and then to watch *Vertigo* and see it play out like that, with the movie's mechanisms somehow decoded for me. I still see that when I watch a movie.

Enablers

CARLA BLUMENKRANZ: When I was trying to make a list of what books have been important to me, I increasingly realized that I have two lists, reading to be a writer versus reading to be a human. Like many people, if I had to say what my favorite book was, I would say *Anna Karenina*. But *Anna Karenina* did not make me want to be a writer.

DAYNA TORTORICI: Which books *did* make you want to be a writer?

CARLA BLUMENKRANZ: Things that were incomplete, things that were short. Because I thought, "Oh, I could write something short." Virginia Woolf's *Between the Acts* was one. That was the only book that has ever made me think, "I want to write a screenplay of this," because I felt, maybe because it was unfinished, that I could get into it more than other things.

EMILY WITT: It took me a long time to admit to myself that I wanted to be a writer, well after college, and I've never wanted to write fiction. So the books that made me want to start writing were after college, when I started reading Joan Didion. I read *The New Journalism* anthology edited by Tom Wolfe. And Ryszard Kapuściński.

DAYNA TORTORICI: Did you stumble onto them, or did you know you wanted to write this way and people told you, "Well, then you should read this stuff"?

EMILY WITT: My dad's a journalist, so in my house it was always like . . . the ideal writer in my house, to my dad, was Jon Krakauer or Sebastian Junger. Super plot-driven, masculine—

EMILY GOULD: Fighting sharks and stuff?

EMILY WITT: Um . . .

EMILY GOULD: And like climbing mountains . . .

EMILY WITT: Yeah, or—

EMILY GOULD: Toting a Kalashnikov . . .

EMILY WITT: I mean, less aesthetic stuff like that, more the idea of a book with intense narrative momentum. So even a Ron Suskind book or—I didn't read this when I was young, but a Katherine Boo book. Nonfiction writing as an immersive reconstructive process. When I read this more self-conscious essay stuff, I felt like I'd found books I felt capable of writing. Still, they are books I consider journalistically "lazy." Didion: great stylist, somewhat lazy reporter. That thing where she talks about how difficult it is for her to make phone calls? Even as I read that with gratitude for her honesty, I also thought, c'mon girl! I have a hang-up that writing about myself is super lazy, whereas the real journalists, through their industry and authority, get paid better to write the book the people want, and they publish immersive, authoritative nonfiction accounts in the *New Yorker* after making a thousand investigative phone calls instead of just forever putting their journal entries in *n+1*.

CARLA BLUMENKRANZ: One thing I remember doing at that age is reading every magazine and every journal all the way through. I didn't think to skip things because I felt I didn't know enough yet to be allowed to skip anything. Did you guys . . . do that?

EMILY GOULD: No, you freak-a-leek! I would just skip around, looking for the sex. Which, in the Tina Brown era of the *New Yorker*, in 1993, was so much sex.

CARLA BLUMENKRANZ: I just felt like there were so many things I didn't know . . . I also hadn't grown up with magazines. I didn't have any context. My parents are great readers, but we didn't have the *New Yorker*. I felt like I was starting from zero. And at some point in college, I subscribed to the *NYRB* and read every article. I didn't know how to skip anything.

DAYNA TORTORICI: Did you have this problem with classes, too? I learned too late in college that you don't have to read everything you're assigned. You can actually put first what's important to you.

EMILY GOULD: It turns out real life is like that, too.

CARLA BLUMENKRANZ: I guess what I'm saying is that it took me a really long time to realize that I didn't have to be a jihadist with everything I did.

EMILY GOULD: Can I go back to "What books made you want to write?"

DAYNA TORTORICI: Yes, please.

EMILY GOULD: The two that I thought of were at different times, and the first was during the Normandy era. She had this book called *The Cutmouth Lady* by Romy Ashby. It was the first book that I ever read in the Semiotext(e) Native Agents Series. It's a novel but not really—it's essays—and they're about an American 14-year-old who's a quarter Japanese and whose parents, for whatever reason, send her to a girls' school in Japan in the late '70s. It's a lot like *Claudine at School*, which I didn't end up reading until a little later. There's a lot of gorgeous, sensual detail and incidental schoolgirl lesbianism. It's just this perfect book. It's really spare, it doesn't feel worked over at all. It seems like a first draft in good and bad ways, but it has this shocking quality that you never find in really commercial first-person writing by women—this quality of just really not giving a fuck. Really, really, really convincingly not caring whether the narrator, the "I," gives the impression of being a good person the reader would want to be pals with. It's not self-deprecating in any way. It's a confession that doesn't ask for forgiveness.

It's not one of the books that endlessly recharges itself, unfortunately. I hope it still has that magic for someone encountering it for the first time, but I think that maybe you have to be 20 and never have read anything like it before. Now of course I've read a lot of things like that. I've made my life about reading things like that. But I think without that book, I'd have never had it in my head that I could write anything.

I Love Dick; Roth; A pile of Kleenex

DAYNA TORTORICI: Did anything particular open up a new world of books or ideas for you?

EMILY GOULD: The book that did it for me was *I Love Dick*. I didn't read it until 2009, and it absolutely changed my life. For many reasons that is the book that changed my life, not in terms of being a writer in any way, but in terms of being a human being and living my life as a mostly heterosexual woman. It explained the problem of heterosexuality to me in terms that I had never thought about before. I had been attracted to books by and about gay people or at least people with fluid sexuality for a long time, and had not spent much time thinking about why that was. Worlds without straight men appealed to me; I liked the idea that there could be narratives that didn't operate on the presumption of women's dependence on men for love, money, and support. *I Love Dick* was the first work of fiction I'd ever read that acknowledged that women who were attracted to men and wanted to have relationships with them were not going to somehow create relationships that existed outside of all existing economic and social structures; that women who love men are going to have to come to terms with their complicity in their own repression and subjugation, and find ways to address it. This is not all the book's about, of course, but that was my first and most lasting takeaway.

But the second thing was, weirdly, around the same time, in my late twenties, I read Philip Roth for the first time. Philip Roth, whom I'd always avoided—along with all the other midcentury misogynists—because I was like, "Nope, can't do it, can't go there. It's bad and un-PC and I won't find anything there that I can stomach. I'll just be so offended and I won't be able to read these books. There are plenty of people enjoying them and I refuse to be one of them."

But it turns out that I love those books. They have that same quality of being unrepentant. And the idea that you can write a novel that very clearly, unabashedly, unrepentantly has autobiographical elements, a novel that says, "What, fuck you, who even cares? This is what a novel is, and you can like it or you can get off the bus"— I appreciated that.

CARLA BLUMENKRANZ: His later books are so craft driven that I don't have a block with them. I think *The Human Stain* is amazing, I think *The Counterlife* is amazing, in a way that doesn't feel particularly different from anything else to me. But his early books—I'm just the worst reader of them. They're the only books where my gender and social life had felt involved in my capacity to read them.

EMILY GOULD: Those are the ones that I'm really into.

CARLA BLUMENKRANZ: The first Roth book I ever read, and one of the very few books I ever read, where I thought, "I don't understand this. It's because I'm a woman. I'm so angry," was *Portnoy's Complaint*. I was 18 or 19. I was not very sexually experienced at all—that's a great understatement—and I didn't understand it, I really did not understand it. I was so upset.

DAYNA TORTORICI: Was it a gendered thing?

CARLA BLUMENKRANZ: No. I mean: I literally did not understand it.

(*Pause.*)

DAYNA TORTORICI: Oh! So it was the first time a book couldn't teach you something—you had to understand sex before you read Roth. Roth couldn't teach you about sex.

CARLA BLUMENKRANZ: It's true. And then I was just depressed. I didn't read him again until after the first serious relationship I had, which wasn't until just after college. My boyfriend was like, "You know, everything that we've been doing together actually is the plot of 'Goodbye Columbus.' You have no idea how much this is just like it." I didn't read it until, inevitably, we broke up two years later, and it was true! I had been such a Brenda. And I'm still a really bad reader of that book.

EMILY WITT: When you say you're a bad reader, you mean you don't like it?

CARLA BLUMENKRANZ: Well, I actually love "Goodbye Columbus," because it turned out that this person I was forcing to go running and eat fruit with me and all of these things was actually replicated in this novella.

EMILY WITT: You saw your own . . .

CARLA BLUMENKRANZ: It was gross. It was horrible.

EMILY WITT: I get kind of irritated or prickly when people say men who write are just creating a fantasy woman, because in fact a male writer can reveal a woman to you in a way that you wouldn't see it. And vice versa. Also, I hate—how do I put this?—the idea that only if a woman is writing with really physical language or using a certain angry tone that she achieves a true female voice, versus . . .

DAYNA TORTORICI: Do people say that?

EMILY WITT: I feel like that's what Emily was just suggesting, kind of. You were referring to commercial women's fiction and being confessional, and I got the sense that you thought it was pretty insipid. And that, you know, *I Love Dick* was a revelation because Chris Kraus was strident.

EMILY GOULD: I don't think that particular distinction was about style.

EMILY WITT: Well, I think we all reach a point in our reading where you start having sex and having relationships, and you need to read about it, because that's how you've always understood the world as a person who reads. And

I hit a wall—for some reason it was hard to find a book that explained what was going on with me in the way that books previously could reflect my reality and help me understand it. *The Bell Jar* was a really important book, and I read that because somebody told me, "This is like *The Catcher in the Rye* for women, from a female perspective." And that was true, for me. That book clarified some of my own thoughts and experiences. But after I read *The Bell Jar* I had trouble finding another bildungsroman by a woman that really resonated with me. I'm not saying they don't exist, but many of the great classic coming-of-age novels about the female experience don't openly discuss sex.

I read the ones by men instead, until I was like, "I cannot read another passage about masturbation. I can't." It was like a pile of Kleenex. I read *Portnoy's Complaint*. I read Jonathan Lethem's *Fortress of Solitude*, when it came out. I read, I don't even remember—but I read like five male coming-of-age novels that had intense, long passages about masturbation. These books taught me a lot about what it must be like to be a young man, and gave me some terrible ideas about the kind of woman I didn't want to be, in order to not be thought dull or needy by the intelligent, masturbating young men I liked, but they did not help me understand my life. Except for *The Bell Jar* I didn't have a book that gave me an archetype, of a young, educated, sexually curious, neurotic but adventurous heterosexual female who was not trying to overcome sexual trauma. I was looking for something at the midpoint between *Anna Karenina* and *Bridget Jones's Diary* and there was just a void. Now I would put Doris Lessing's *The Golden Notebook* in there, and Zadie Smith's *NW*.

EMILY GOULD: Go back to the thing you were saying earlier, about how you get upset when people say male novelists aren't able to portray women.

EMILY WITT: Well, the pernicious thing about reading Roth when you're a young person is that you think, "I don't want to be that girlfriend. I don't want to act like that." Because the men around me were speaking that language when I read those books, that was how I reacted. I thought, "This is a world that I have to conform to." And I still haven't resolved whether that's true or not. It may be true.

CARLA BLUMENKRANZ: You mean a world where everyone reads Roth, or a world in which sexual dynamics are as they are portrayed there?

EMILY WITT: The sexual dynamics. In college, you're reading, but you're also having really intense personal experiences, right? You're really having sex for the first time, really dating for the first time, and you're looking for things to help you understand it. I had a boyfriend that I found out had been to prostitutes. I had a boyfriend that cheated on me. Stuff that in these novels *is* adulthood. These were the books that were handed to me, and so I thought, "This is something that I have to get used to." I knew that if I had been a young man, I would mimic these novels too. The realization that there were parts of that acting out that I didn't get to do, solely because of my gender, and other parts in which my acting out was seen differently, not as fun but desperate, was devastating. I can't even explain how devastating that was. I couldn't even think of the ethics of any of it because all I saw was the role I was confined to in those stories. I can't think of a book that I would've given myself that would've armed me against that feeling. I got really mad at the books. I remember getting mad at a boyfriend who had lied and saying, "YOU THINK YOU'RE THE HERO OF A FUCKING UPDIKE NOVEL." But it was my role I resented, the role of the bovine female, while he was the Julien Sorel, the deceptive, neurotic, charmingly flawed hero balancing competing claims for his affection— again, the bearer of narrative.

DAYNA TORTORICI: Can't rejecting a certain kind of novel be a way of rejecting a certain kind of reality? I think that's why I never wanted to read Roth. My feeling was, "I don't want to live in a world in which this mirrors reality."

EMILY WITT: But when a Roth-like situation is really happening to you . . .

DAYNA TORTORICI: . . . then it's important to read Roth?

EMILY WITT: It is. And that's why reading Foucault was super important to me in college. *The History of Sexuality* talks a lot about confession and the power bestowed upon the person who receives the confession. The reason that Roth felt like something that I had to conform to was that I couldn't go to a prostitute. There was nothing that I could do that would make a man feel the way that I had been made to feel. This was a fact of being alive I had to conform to. When I read Foucault, he explained the dynamic: that being able to know a world, and bear its secrets, is a kind of power over somebody. And forbidding access to that kind of knowledge—of being able to look at somebody sexually in that way, or to purchase a sexual body, even just going to a strip club—there's a power that exists there. There wasn't a novel that I could've read that would've helped me. Or maybe there is one. I don't know.

The secret canon

EMILY GOULD: I used to be really into comic books, and I dip back into them occasionally. I'll get sick of novels and other kinds of book-books, and then I'll refresh myself in a cleansing mikveh of comics. One series I started reading when I was a sophomore in high school, and continued to read, is *Love and Rockets*. It doesn't fit in with any of my other hobby-horse things, but I love the idea of serialization. I hope that it could happen again. I read *Enemies, A Love Story* for the first time semi-recently, and I was like, "Oh, I see, if you can't sustain your interest in writing a scene for longer than an hour it's OK, because you can just have a lot of scenes that are about fifteen hundred words long."

DAYNA TORTORICI: I just read that this spring! I loved that book.

CARLA BLUMENKRANZ: I'm so glad, now I get to introduce my concept of the secret canon.

DAYNA TORTORICI: The secret canon?

CARLA BLUMENKRANZ: Because *Enemies, A Love Story* is clearly in the secret canon of this book! It's in the first one as well—Becky Curtis mentions it.*

EMILY WITT: What is the secret canon?

---

* See *What We Should Have Known*, 38.

CARLA BLUMENKRANZ: Whenever you're put in a university or even just in a group of people, there's always a secret canon that everyone's referring to.

DAYNA TORTORICI: What makes the secret canon canonical? That so many people have managed to read it? Or that everything in it is good?

CARLA BLUMENKRANZ: It's just a reference point. There's a collection of books that will tell you so much about the microculture you're in, and that's the secret canon. When I first came to *n+1*, I thought, "Oh no. All these people went to Harvard and they have an entirely different secret canon than I do."

DAYNA TORTORICI: But the secret canon of Harvard is just the canon!

EMILY GOULD: Like the Frankfurt School?

CARLA BLUMENKRANZ: Yeah, things I had maybe gotten an excerpt from in college but had never read seriously. All of a sudden it seemed like I had to read these things really quickly, because I was in this new place with a new canon. Arbitrary things, too.

DAYNA TORTORICI: What books belong to Carla's concept of the secret canon, in your social worlds? Books that everyone seems to have read?

EMILY WITT: For me, it's often the actual canon. When I went to Cambridge, I saw that in England the Western canon is very alive and intact. But in general I always read books because of people I'm making friends with. It's the main way I get book knowledge.

EMILY GOULD: I like the secret canon idea so much. Establishing your group of friends is about establishing a canon among you. When you want to be friends with somebody, your interest is really real. My two book-recommending friends are both people I met when we were prepubescent, Normandy and Bennet. Normandy's a playwright and Bennet is a novelist. Early in college, when I moved to New York, Bennet and I both read this book that I tried to reread recently and can't—it's un-rereadable—but I loved it so much then, *In the City of Shy Hunters* by Tom Spanbauer. It made us both want to move to the East Village, which we did, and it made us want to intern for its publisher, which we both did, with completely life-altering results for both of us.

DAYNA TORTORICI: Do you regret reading it?

EMILY GOULD: I guess not! Now I think it's corny. It's '80s East Village with elements of, um, (*wincing*) magical realism. Not the kind of thing that I would pick up today, but it really resonated with 19-year-old me. But, yes, I have relationships that have a canon unto themselves, and a constant stream of recommendations that go back and forth, and I'm mostly talking about the back—people recommending things to me. I see myself as a malleable repository of other people's tastes.

DAYNA TORTORICI: And yet you are such the opposite. I mean, *I Love Dick* belongs to the secret canon, in my mind, because of you.

CARLA BLUMENKRANZ: What secret canon are you referring to?

DAYNA TORTORICI: I don't know. The secret canon in my life that I know and read.

EMILY WITT: Ugh, I couldn't get through it.

DAYNA TORTORICI: Really?

CARLA BLUMENKRANZ: Yeah . . .

EMILY GOULD: It does have a slow start. I tell people—this is what my friend Ruth told me, when she recommended it to me. She said, "Bear with it for the first half. You'll be really irritated and it'll seem really pretentious to you."

EMILY WITT: The first *half*?

EMILY GOULD: The first half.

EMILY WITT: That's a lot of the book.

EMILY GOULD: It's worth it.

EMILY WITT: Huh.

CARLA BLUMENKRANZ: (*murmuring*)

DAYNA TORTORICI: What's up?

CARLA BLUMENKRANZ: Oh, I just, I think, um . . . You all have interpreted the secret canon in much nicer ways than me.

DAYNA TORTORICI: Oh! That was a mistake. Tell us what it actually means?

CARLA BLUMENKRANZ: No, no, it's great to think of books as being part of your social life. I guess it's never quite been that way for me. When I first became interested in the Literary Arts program at Brown, it seemed like the people there lived in a world of experimental literature, were gateways to it, and I had to find it all and read it all. I went straight from that to *n+1*, which was, you know, a group of people who spoke about canonical works, bigger works. And I felt I had to figure all these things out.

DAYNA TORTORICI: So you thought of it more as a set of social prerequisites.

CARLA BLUMENKRANZ: I guess I had a colder view of things, which is not quite as nice as the idea of living in the world of people and books together.

EMILY WITT: Not having had the Western canon and then encountering situations where I needed to have a fluency in it, I saw how the canon can be used—and probably the secret canon, all canons—as shorthand for intelligence. Even though the easiest thing in the world is to tell a smart person to read a book. A lot of times the canon is instead mistaken for capability, and awareness of the world, knowledge of the world.

CARLA BLUMENKRANZ: Yes, I think that's more what I meant. Not a feat of strength, but fluency.

———

Sylvia Plath; Big, messy books; Janet Malcolm

EMILY GOULD: A couple of years ago I was assigned to write two thousand words about the anniversary of *The Bell Jar*. I hadn't read it since high school, and I reread it, and a bunch of books around it, many Plath bios, including Janet Malcolm's *The Silent Woman*, which is a completely fascinating book in and of itself. It has a crazy, crazy moment, crazy in a good way, that's about what every Janet Malcolm book is about, to some extent—fights over who gets to be in charge of the truth about someone's life.

The Bell Jar became important to me for a bunch of reasons. I was surprised at how great a framework it is for so many other books, and how many other books are varying degrees of good copies of it. And it became clear, from reading the biographical literature around it, that it wasn't an upwelling of someone's soul. It was rather: Plath sees that someone very famous and successful has written a memoir of being in a mental institution, and it was a real financial windfall for her. She was like, "I've got that in my wheelhouse, I'm just gonna do that, too, I'll crank it out this summer." And that is what she did.

It was also instructive to think of that book as a part of someone's career that did not meet with instantaneous acclaim. This is a cliché, but the book initially got very bad reviews, was met with *meh*s all around. It was actually reviewed so badly that, you know—there were other things going on—but, you know, she killed herself, obviously. It was a good moment for me to read that book and to have to write about it, because the themes of the book felt so eternally relevant. It's a great book and fun to read, and I recommend it to everyone who hasn't read it since they were 14, which is really too young to understand it.

CARLA BLUMENKRANZ: One book I read recently that I admired a whole lot, and that made me rethink some things, was *The Age of Innocence*. It has a generosity that I look for in novels a lot more recently, I think, that she didn't have in her early books. There's a warmth to it. It doesn't have the sort of social rage that *The House of Mirth* has, but a kind of generosity I really admire.

DAYNA TORTORICI: When you say "generosity," what exactly do you mean?

CARLA BLUMENKRANZ: It's not angry at its time, there's not a suicide at the end. It's an interesting experiment for me to think about a novel that's fundamentally tolerant of the social norms that it depicts.

Also, people that I read a little earlier who I think are my idea of perfection are Virginia Woolf, for probably the reasons many people say, and Chekhov, because they contain and sometimes resolve a lot of what I struggle with, which is how to let life in and let people in while also retaining an idealism about literature itself. With Chekhov, you feel that the writer is often very tolerant of human failings, of varying types of characters, of characters who are like him.

EMILY WITT: There's books that mattered to me because I wanted to be a writer, and then books that I just love. For philosophy, *The History of Sexuality* and *The Order of Things* were really important to me, and Barthes's *S/Z*. It's a brilliant disassembly of how texts work, and it's just really satisfying. It's so contained in these really nice little prisms, like a game.

These aren't the books that I think are the best books in the world, I just like big books, but *Moby-Dick*, *Gravity's Rainbow*, *Infinite Jest*, *The Golden Notebook*. They're all big, messy books. I'm into nonfiction, so I guess Didion. I don't know why I'm reluctant to say Didion except that she also annoys me. I feel like I can't escape her. She imposes a certain model that a lot of things get thrown into. Still, it's an approach that obviously influenced how I write nonfiction. William Finnegan is to me a perfect journalist. He's not there but he's there.

DAYNA TORTORICI: What are some titles?

EMILY WITT: His first book is called *Crossing the Line*, about teaching in South Africa during apartheid. And the second one is about the Mozambican civil war, called *A Complicated War.* The third one I don't like as much, it's called the *Cold New World*, and it's about urban poverty. But really just read his *New Yorker* archive, most of which is not in books. Read an article called "The Last Tour."

DAYNA TORTORICI: Emily Gould, what about you?

EMILY GOULD: Um . . . I guess two books about AIDS. One, *The Gentrification of the Mind* by Sarah Schulman. The other, *Chronicle of a Plague, Revisited,* by Andrew Holleran. They both describe a generation and a world that was lost, and I think if you are younger than a certain age you don't even really have an ambient awareness that this was a huge deal, that this whole group of people who might be peers and mentors are missing from the world. And purely as books I would recommend them, too.

A book that I read when I was somewhere around college age was *Chelsea Girls* by Eileen Myles. I don't remember what struck me so much about it—probably the same stuff that I've been saying for hours now, about a styleless style that seems effortless and unforced and doesn't give a fuck, that reports without judgment.

I also don't want to leave without mentioning that I once had a job where my boss said, "Oh, you haven't read *The Journalist and the Murderer*? Here, take it, don't come back to work until you've finished it."

DAYNA TORTORICI: What's that?

EVERYONE: Janet Malcolm!

EMILY GOULD: I only read like half of it. But even if you only read the first page and a half, that's an important takeaway—

EMILY WITT: Why did you stop reading it?

EMILY GOULD: Oh, I don't know. I lost interest in what it was actually about.

EMILY WITT: I stopped reading it because I was like, "Yeah, anybody who's ever been a journalist has had to deal with this fact that you're manipulating people and you're a succubus of their stories." To me, it was too obvious.

CARLA BLUMENKRANZ: I recently reread a lot of Janet Malcolm, and yeah—I think her thesis is in the first few pages of that book.

DAYNA TORTORICI: What do they say?

CARLA BLUMENKRANZ: What Emily Witt said, basically. I think she's in the best sense a phenomenally moral writer. She thinks about how one ought to treat people and how narrative is in conflict with that constantly, in all her books. *The Journalist and the Murderer* is probably the most straightforward example of that. *The Silent Woman* is probably the most complex.

EMILY GOULD: I think certainly there are people who want to be nonfiction writers who are younger, who have not yet grappled with how their writing might affect other people's lives. It's probably a good path to go down no matter how you get there, whether it's that book or some other experience you have. It might be good to have an intimation of that prior to, you know—

EMILY WITT: Learning it the hard way.

CARLA BLUMENKRANZ: This is kind of a Malcolm-like thing to worry about, but I think especially as a reader, you tend to trust your own instincts and to read exactly what you want to read and to do exactly what you think is good for you—but I wish I had done more reading against myself. Maybe that's too hard to do. But I wish I had done more to counter my own forms of extremism earlier than I did. You know, I wish that when I wanted everything to be as difficult and spare as it could be, that I had the self-knowledge to also be pursuing things that were bigger and easier. But that might be too hard. +

GROUP THREE

September 21, 2013

Elif Batuman (New York, NY, 1977)
Elizabeth Gumport (New York, NY, 1985)
Amanda Katz (Boston, MA, 1978)
Namara Smith (Arlington, VA, 1986)
Astra Taylor (Winnipeg, MB, Canada, 1979)

DAYNA TORTORICI: I'll start with a question I've asked all of the groups, a yes-or-no question with qualifications allowed. Do you have regrets about college? What you did, how you were?

ELIZABETH GUMPORT: Yes and no. Yes, in that I do, and no in that if I let myself have them, I'd regret everything. So no.

ASTRA TAYLOR: No, no regrets.

AMANDA KATZ: I think not really. I could have done something different, and that could have been good, too, but I love what I did in college.

NAMARA SMITH: Yes and no, too.

ELIF BATUMAN: Well yeah, I think that's the only answer that makes any sense. Because you don't . . . I mean you don't know what would have hap— . . . how could you regret someth—

ELIZABETH GUMPORT: It makes no sense.

ELIF BATUMAN: Exactly. So, yeah: No.

_____

Wrong science; Office hours

DAYNA TORTORICI: When you were 18, what ideas did you have about yourself and what you wanted to do?

ELIF BATUMAN: I definitely wanted to be a writer. But I thought that to become a writer you should never read any books and not write at all, so I started out in linguistics.

DAYNA TORTORICI: Never read any books . . . ?

ELIF BATUMAN: Because if you read too many books you would have problems writing. I grew up during the cold war, and you were supposed to be creative, unlike the people in the Soviet Union, who read books. It was all about not reading books and having untrammeled creativity. At the same time, you had to be doing something, and linguistics seemed like it was contentless enough to not get in the way of my creativity, and it was still kind of language-related. You couldn't study literature either, because this was the tail end of the vogue for deconstruction, and if you did that too much you would destroy your ability to write—because you would know too much, you would know how things worked, and then you would be unable to write with the starry, naive romantic creativity you were striving for. Linguistics seemed irrelevant enough to not interfere with that.

DAYNA TORTORICI: How long did you stick with it?

ELIF BATUMAN: Like a month maybe.

DAYNA TORTORICI: Then what happened?

ELIF BATUMAN: Well, then I got into Russian literature. But it was the same thing, because I was just studying Russian. Russian is such a hard language, I just spent all of college trying to learn Russian. So when I say a month, I mean more like a year. I spent a year in linguistics and then I switched to literature, but I spent the whole time studying Russian language. And doing random pointless stuff that had no point.

NAMARA SMITH: I don't think I had enough ideas about myself. I never had to decide where to go to college or what to study. When I was 15, I already knew I would go to this small liberal arts college, because my dad taught there and it was free. It had a set curriculum, so I never had to choose any courses. I spent a lot of time learning about things like Ptolemaic geometry, which I sometimes regret because it was wrong.

ELIF BATUMAN: It's true, it's just wrong.

NAMARA SMITH: I learned a lot of things that were wrong, especially in math and science.

DAYNA TORTORICI: Were they taught to you as if they were true?

NAMARA SMITH: No, just as part of the history of science and as examples of systems of thought. How Ptolemy's astronomy is so perfect in some ways, because it fits with the intuitive experience of seeing the sun move in the sky, but how you have to keep adding deferents and epicycles and retrograde motion to make it work.

ELIF BATUMAN: Was this a really progressive school?

NAMARA SMITH: It was the Great Books program at St. John's. In some ways it was really progressive. There were no tests, all the classes were discussion-based, and we weren't supposed to look at our grades. But in other ways it was really conservative—I mean, we questioned the value of the Copernican revolution.

I guess my idea of myself was that Ptolemy was really interesting.

AMANDA KATZ: My feelings about what I was doing and what I'm doing now are almost disturbingly unchanged. Even in high school, I was trying to train myself to figure out how writing worked—to break it down into smaller and smaller pieces, to understand how certain kinds of writing achieved the effects they did. I majored in comparative literature with a focus on literary translation. All my work since has been about figuring out how the structure of writing works on the micro or macro scale; I'm a poet but I'm mostly a book editor. But then my education outside writing was actually totally scattershot—sort of the opposite of a Great Books program. When I look back, I'm like, My god, it's all holes.

NAMARA SMITH: But I feel that way about my education, too.

AMANDA KATZ: Really, even though you had that Great Books structure?

NAMARA SMITH: But it stopped in like 1930 . . . I think the last book that I read was *Mrs Dalloway.*

AMANDA KATZ: That was where it ended?

NAMARA SMITH: I read one early Derrida book, and that was it. And then I was released into the world.

ELIF BATUMAN: College is so short, whatever collection of stuff you read just seems super arbitrary. Like, why did I read André Breton in college, why? You read stuff that's been curated in little semester-long groups, and you go through eight of them and then you're done.

ELIZABETH GUMPORT: I wish I'd had more people trying to make me do things. Giving me advice, if only so I could reject it. About what to read, what classes to take, anything, just so I could say no, or have a sense of what people thought I should do.

DAYNA TORTORICI: Did you feel like you were supposed to be doing something?

ELIZABETH GUMPORT: I don't think so, but people were getting advice.

ELIF BATUMAN: I remember envying people who were getting advice. I had one friend in particular who just got a lot of advice.

ELIZABETH GUMPORT: What kind of advice, and from whom?

ELIF BATUMAN: She was this fabulous Serbian refugee whose dad was legal counsel for Coca-Cola in Yugoslavia, they had a ton of money, and she had a shrink who was obsessed with her because she was this extremely interesting case. Also a French tutor whose whole job was to read decadent French poems with her and then they would make fun of decadence, in French. And she would go to office hours—which is something I actually had huge contempt for, I thought that you had to be a weak, deficient person to do it. Why would I envy her? I don't know. She had all these people who seemed tremendously concerned with her intellectual development, in a Henry James-y kind of way. And she would tell me things they said about her, like, "So-and-so said I'm the kind of person who's like X, so I should do Y," and part of me would think it sounded self-dramatizing and childish. And part of me would be like, "That must be amazing."

I guess I had this idea about myself that I was the kind of person who does not receive advice.

NAMARA SMITH: But what is the sort of person that goes to office hours and gets advice?

AMANDA KATZ: Yeah, why did you have contempt for office hours?

ELIF BATUMAN: I had huge contempt! If I regret anything it's that I never went to office hours. I didn't have a relationship with any professor. So when it was time to write a thesis, I didn't have a faculty adviser; I was randomly assigned to a lecturer, who turned out to be a truly astounding teacher, and had a hugely positive effect on my life, and she modified my bad attitude. But she didn't totally get rid of it, because she seemed so sort of frail and exploited. She was Polish, and she had done a PhD in English at Cornell and her area was I think Hardy and James and belatedness, and instead of getting a research faculty position in an English department, she was on this really tough three-year contract at Harvard, in the undergrad comp lit department, where she ended up having to deal with all the Russian language majors who didn't have an adviser. She was, like, running kind of a Russian orphanage—and she *hated* Russians, because the only reason she knew Russian was because they occupied her country and made her speak Russian for her whole university education. She could still remember the times when sugar was rationed: she would be like, "We only had two kilograms of sugar a month . . . !"

I was so sad when she said that, though later I thought: "That's, like, four pounds of sugar!"

Anyway, I felt like she and I were this team. It was her and me against everyone else. I felt that way with my boyfriend, too, and that's just the idea I had of myself. Looking back, I really didn't need to feel so embattled. I got over it eventually, but I wish it hadn't lasted as long, or been so extreme. I wish I had, you know, taken survey classes in college, and not felt antagonized by the idea that people were trying to teach me stuff. I took one survey class, freshman year, because the woman who was my assigned adviser—a different one; she worked in the telephone office and had no connection to Harvard except . . .

ELIZABETH GUMPORT: What's the telephone office?

ELIF BATUMAN: It doesn't exist anymore. You wouldn't know about it. Ask your parents, there was something called the office of telephone communications. I forget what they did, but she worked there. She was Scottish, I think, and she had done a PhD at Harvard in Old Norse, in the '70s. She told me to take this survey class with a famous Slavist, and I just hated it. The lectures seemed like he was just informing us how brilliant and subtle the authors were, without talking about what they meant— like his job was to make sure we came out with good taste and weren't philistines. At the end, students asked questions. They would ask what I thought were really clear questions, and he never seemed to understand what they were saying. So he would give a weird answer that seemed not at all related to the question, and the worst part was this look on his face . . .

DAYNA TORTORICI: What was the look?

ELIF BATUMAN: Kind of a smile, a squinty smile, like a ghastly simulacrum of fun. He wasn't a bad guy or anything—when I did junior semester abroad in Russia, he had to approve my plan of study, and he was really kind and reasonable. I just found that lecture class really upsetting. And when you're young and don't have that many experiences, you overvalue each experience—so I didn't think, "This is a guy whose teaching style I don't appreciate." Instead I thought, "This is the great Harvard University and it has nothing to tell me about books, I'm on my own with the books, it's just me and them." For years it didn't occur to me that other people could help me in the search for meaning, that it's actually a collaborative enterprise. So I think I missed a lot of opportunities.

Also, when I was growing up, this was before the internet, and whenever we were sitting at the table and someone wanted to know something, my mom would be like, "Oh, let's call Marshall." Marshall was this very sophisticated older gay guy who lived on the West Side somewhere—we lived in New Jersey—and he had an amazing book collection, and he really did know a lot of stuff, but I would just . . .

AMANDA KATZ: So he was the internet?

ELIF BATUMAN: Yes, he was the internet! Someone would have a question about books, or music, or art, or New York, and they would be like, "We should call Marshall!" And they would call Marshall and ask him. He must have been a remarkably patient guy. But I remember thinking, "Isn't there just a book that I can look it up in, instead of calling this guy?" The idea of fetishizing some baby-boomer guy who has the information you need was distasteful to me. So I didn't go to office hours.

Unschooling; Competition; Excellence as distraction

ASTRA TAYLOR: At 18, I guess I was already over college, and on my way out.

AMANDA KATZ: Did you start at 12?

ASTRA TAYLOR: Well, sort of, because I was unschooled,* so I had an unusual relationship to education. At 18, I'd already figured out how to exit Brown and graduate.

DAYNA TORTORICI: You were a freshman and you figured out how to graduate?

ASTRA TAYLOR: Yeah. I'd had a moment when I was about 17 when I thought, "OK, I should compete like everybody else, I should go to Brown and I should be a physicist." And so I spent a year at Brown as a math major, studying calculus and physics. I took a cognitive science class and I hated it. I hated everything about it. I never went to office hours. I barely went to class. The thing I did master was the logic of this system, and I figured out that I could go back to Georgia and I could graduate the next year. I thought it would be a smart thing to have a degree, and there were some people at the University of Georgia that I could study with, so that's what I did.

It was there that I decided that I could continue my unschooling as an adult and just do the things that I was interested in—thinking about politics and social change and philosophy. So at that age I'd broken free of the sense that I should be doing the regular academic

---

*See "Unschooling" by Astra Taylor in *n+1* Issue Thirteen, "Machine Politics." Unschooling differs from homeschooling in that it doesn't try to replicate school at home.

trajectory, much to the relief of my parents. I remember my dad saying that he was so happy that I got "the silly Ivy League thing out of my system." At 18 I had come full circle and decided that it was OK, I could just be who I was when I was 8 years old. That was sort of the beginning of my adult life, and my day-to-day activities haven't really changed much since then.

DAYNA TORTORICI: Why did you think you should be a physicist at Brown?

ASTRA TAYLOR: I think because it seemed hard, and because it seemed comfortingly objective. I had gotten myself into this incredible existential funk as a child about moral relativity and animal rights—I had a crazy animal rights and environmental magazine and was pathologically invested in it, and also completely convinced that I was going to start a revolution among young people, like other 10- and 11-year-olds. But when I went to public high school I realized that not everyone agreed with me. Everyone wasn't a crazy hippie. I thought, "How do I know I'm right and everybody's wrong?" And so I turned to the sciences. It's also where you get that feedback loop, academically: positive reinforcement, good grades, stuff like that, and it's so easy to climb. That was something completely new to me, having grades, having gold stars. I got into that.

So those were the two bizarre motivations that led me to science. By the time I got back to UGA, though, I realized that whatever I wanted to do in the evening I should be doing during the day. And if the university was a resource I ended up utilizing, and if there were knowledgeable people that I was inspired by who were professors or mentors, then that'd be great. But I completely disconnected from the identity of a student.

ELIZABETH GUMPORT: Who were the mentors that you found?

ASTRA TAYLOR: When I was 17 I saw somebody reading *A Thousand Plateaus* by Deleuze and Guattari—I was really intrigued by this book—and it turned out that in Athens, Georgia, my little podunk town that I really wanted to leave so badly, the first American to write a book on Deleuze and Guattari taught at the university. So I went and emailed this guy. He was great, and I took an amazing grad seminar he offered where we just read that book. That was a really formative experience. And then this amazing woman who was kind of a poststructuralist literary theorist . . . She led me astray in a lot of ways, but she was a model of a female intellectual that I'd never really seen before, and I think she was grateful to have a student who was so eager. I didn't stay the four years, though.

ELIZABETH GUMPORT: Four years is kind of the worst amount of time. College should be a year. Or a hundred years.

ASTRA TAYLOR: It should be a hundred years!

DAYNA TORTORICI: Elizabeth, what about you? What were your ideas about yourself?

ELIZABETH GUMPORT: I think . . . not enough. And I think that I knew that, and avoided it by letting myself be really competitive. My school didn't have grades until high school, and when we did I loved it. In college I felt the same way. I avoided thinking about what I wanted to do by competing instead. So I'd think, "I'm going to tap out of math, I'm not going to win that." That was a mistake, but it was also a mistake I would have made no matter what.

DAYNA TORTORICI: Presumably your attitude changed at some point, in college.

ELIZABETH GUMPORT: Never entirely, I don't think.

Reading men in foreign places

DAYNA TORTORICI: Where did you get cues about what to read? Elizabeth, I remember you telling me once about your first stint in grad school—how you went for English, and you were really into some poet . . .

ELIZABETH GUMPORT: Romantic poets.

DAYNA TORTORICI: You were really into Romantic poets, but really only because of this one influential teacher—

ELIZABETH GUMPORT: Paul Fry.

DAYNA TORTORICI: Right, and once you got to your PhD program, you realized, "Wait, I don't give a shit about Romantic poets, I just had that one teacher who made me love Romantic poets." Can you say more about that?

ELIZABETH GUMPORT: I feel like it was a past life. All of these things seem like past lives. There were teachers, but a lot of the cues were the wrong ones. I guess that's what I meant when I said I wish more people had given me advice, so at least I could know why I did the things that I did or didn't do. But I have no idea . . . I just don't know.

DAYNA TORTORICI: But what *did* you do?

ELIZABETH GUMPORT: What did I read? Well, in high school I had a really significant teacher, and he was really into Joyce and Pynchon, so I read all of Joyce.

ELIF BATUMAN: I already hate this guy.

ELIZABETH GUMPORT: And my senior year I did an independent project on *Gravity's Rainbow*. I was 17; that's not what I would advise any 17-year-old to do. But it's what I did. I regret that, but I don't regret reading *The Crying of Lot 49*.

NAMARA SMITH: I took *Gravity's Rainbow* with me to Kinshasa, in the DRC, when I was consulting there for two months. That was the wrong book to read there. And I didn't even read most of it, I just read the sex scenes, which are terrible.

ELIZABETH GUMPORT: That's such a funny book to read the sex scenes for, because it's so hard to tell the difference between those and any other scene.

DAYNA TORTORICI: What were you doing there?

NAMARA SMITH: I was working for a consulting company, doing admin work, which was mostly procurement, finding furniture for all their regional offices. They had four regional offices, and I had to buy their desks at a good price and find out how to send them to all these places, which is terrible in the Congo because they don't have any roads, so you have to find a boat or get it on an airplane. In any case, I should have brought something that wasn't so masculine and depressing and crazy. I think that when you're in a crazy situation, you shouldn't read something that's also crazy.

DAYNA TORTORICI: How did you end up with this job?

NAMARA SMITH: It was work that my mom was doing. I didn't know what I wanted to do after I left school, at all, because I had made no choices up to the point when I graduated.

ASTRA TAYLOR: I had an oddly analogous situation where I spent six weeks in southern Senegal, working on a project about infant malnutrition. It was the only time I really read modernist literature; I brought Beckett's trilogy, I read *Ulysses*, I read all of *Capital*, Volume 1. And I read *Absalom, Absalom!* I don't really read literature, but I found, being so disoriented and also involved in this quest, *We must find starving infants, we must document, we must film*—we were working for an NGO—to retreat into this fictional world of male classic angst and stuff, it really worked for me in that context.

ELIF BATUMAN: I had the worst time ever trying to read Henry Miller in Samarkand. I had a serious crush on a guy who said that *Sexus*, *Plexus*, and *Nexus* were the best books ever, so I went to a bookstore, and they were too expensive, so I just got *Sexus* and *Plexus*. And I brought them with me to Samarkand. I felt so alienated by the books, and then thinking about this guy, and it was so hot and summertime . . . I just wanted to kill myself. Then I didn't know what to do with the books, because they had these naked ladies on the cover. I think I wrapped them in paper and put them in the garbage.

ASTRA TAYLOR: You didn't identify with Mona or whatever her name is?

ELIF BATUMAN: I didn't get far enough, I just remember all of this hot soup gushing on his hand in the back of taxicabs, and roaches, there were a lot of roaches. He compared women to soup.

AMANDA KATZ: Soup?

ELIF BATUMAN: Soup.

ELIZABETH GUMPORT: I haven't read any Henry Miller and I don't care.

NAMARA SMITH: Yeah, I don't feel guilty about that at all.

DAYNA TORTORICI: If you change your mind, I know of some copies in a garbage can in Samarkand.

ELIF BATUMAN: You're going to have to look hard, though, because they're wrapped up pretty good.

Shiksa ice queens; Dickens, Firestone

DAYNA TORTORICI: What about books that you didn't read, sooner or at all, based on some sort of personal bias?

ELIF BATUMAN: I didn't read anything American, because that was what was taught in high school and middle school, and in such a horrible way. I never read anything by Faulkner, because we read "A Rose for Emily," a horrible dreadful story taught in a dreadful way.

Also, my mother's boyfriend really liked Philip Roth, and I hated him. He thought he was like Philip Roth, he talked about shiksas and ice queens, and then he dumped my mom for a shiksa ice queen who spent all his money and bought a house in Vermont, and he dropped dead riding a bicycle around Martha's Vineyard. He used to call my mother and complain about the shiksa ice queen, "She doesn't like to eat dinner, she eats cereal on the treadmill!" And that's why I didn't read Philip Roth until this year. This year I read *American Pastoral*. It's really good.

AMANDA KATZ: I should have read more Dickens earlier. I feel like everyone complains about, "Oh, in high school you have to read all this Dickens." But nobody assigned me any Dickens!

ELIF BATUMAN: It's perfect for kids.

AMANDA KATZ: It's perfect for kids, and it would've been helpful for me when I was understanding how novels work. I read *Bleak House* last year, and thought, "This book is amazing! People should really read this great book, *Bleak House*."

ASTRA TAYLOR: It's really interesting, as somebody who's not particularly interested in fiction or writing fiction, to talk about novels in terms of "I should have read." For me the idea that there are novels out there that I'll read later in life and enjoy is a great thing; it's like thinking there are bands out there I'll discover, there's more pleasure to be had. They are exercises in escape, and if there's some sort of lesson about human nature, some sort of role modeling or something, then it's a bonus.

AMANDA KATZ: What drives you to read things now?

ASTRA TAYLOR: Usually now there's something I want to understand in the world, and then it's nonfiction, typically. There's an instrumentality to it.

DAYNA TORTORICI: Can you name some books that were instrumental to you, in some way, when you were college-aged?

ASTRA TAYLOR: *Capital*, and *A Thousand Plateaus*. Certainly, novels that had a feeling about them. When I was 18 or 19 I really liked *The Passion According to G. H.* by Clarice Lispector, about a woman and a cockroach. It had this kind of mood that I liked. But, often it was books that were portals into other reading, books that inspired me to seek out more books. *A Thousand Plateaus* led me to Marx and Lacan and Freud and Beckett and all these things. I was looking for stepping-stones to other books.

DAYNA TORTORICI: Other people?

ELIZABETH GUMPORT: *Daring to Be Bad* by Alice Echols, *The Dialectic of Sex* by Shulamith Firestone, all of the *Notes from the Second Year*, all of the writings by the radical feminists. I wish I had read them earlier. I read them at what feels like the exact right moment, but probably I would have felt it was the right moment even years before that.

ASTRA TAYLOR: I look at *Gender Trouble*, which many argue is not a well-written book, but when I read that as a teenager—

ELIF BATUMAN: That book did nothing for me, nothing.

ASTRA TAYLOR: Really? If I reread it now I don't think it would do as much. But it just seemed so refreshing and inspiring then, such a welcome change from the earth-mother-thank-the-goddess essentialist feminism I was raised with.

ELIF BATUMAN: I was probably too old when I read it. It was in a grad school seminar, and it felt misplaced.

ASTRA TAYLOR: It's a teenager's book, maybe.

ELIF BATUMAN: Yeah, and it had to compete with so much. In that seminar, Fredric Jameson just made my head explode and I had no time for anyone else.

ASTRA TAYLOR: It's interesting that all that second-wave feminist writing feels revelatory for people who are just out of college. I think it shows that *Gender Trouble* is more often taught than *The Dialectic of Sex*.

ELIF BATUMAN: I've never heard of that, what is that?

DAYNA TORTORICI: It's Shulamith Firestone.

ELIF BATUMAN: I've never read that.

DAYNA TORTORICI: It's a radical feminist book from the 1970s, one of the core movement texts. Shulamith Firestone wrote it when she was 25, and you get the impression, reading it, that she wrote it in a fever, in one sitting. It's interesting because—people disagree about this—but it's not a *good* book, exactly. The beginning is just brilliant. It has this great first line, "Sex class is so deep as to be invisible." But then there's all sorts of crazy stuff, like this one chapter on race where she tries to map Freud's Oedipal triangle onto race relations in America, to understand the relationship between white women and black men as oppressed people—so the white man is the father and the white woman, the mother, and the black man, the child. It just goes off the rails in this sloppy, racist way. And then at one point she says something like, "There has never been a woman scientist."

ASTRA TAYLOR: Did she say that?

DAYNA TORTORICI: She says, "One would have to search to find even one woman who had contributed in a major way to scientific culture."

AMANDA KATZ: In what sense has there never been a woman scientist?

DAYNA TORTORICI: I mean, I'm paraphrasing—but I think, if we're being generous, in the sense that women lack institutional recognition and therefore get left out of history. For her, saying there has never been a woman scientist is a way of saying that scientists are made not by doing science but by being recognized as scientists. Still, it reads like she's saying, "no woman has ever contributed to scientific culture." Which is wrong, obviously.

I don't mean to knock this book—it's really ingenious and inspired in other ways, and it was a totally game-changing piece of feminist thinking, for history and for me personally. It's also really funny. *Dialectic of Sex* is a really funny book! I think it's a shame that no one ever mentions that.

ASTRA TAYLOR: It also creates the model of the crazed young female intellectual that you have never seen before. As a role model, she is totally mind-blowing to people.

DAYNA TORTORICI: Yes, she blew my mind. She was majorly important to me. The stuff she says about love and heterosexuality and the culture of romance is perfect. "Down with Childhood" is perfect. She argues that the liberation of women depends on the liberation of children.

ELIF BATUMAN: It's so true.

NAMARA SMITH: I wish I had read that when I was 19.

ELIF BATUMAN: I just read *I Love Dick* for the first time and I wish I had read that sooner. I like that book a lot.

ASTRA TAYLOR: What do you think you would have gotten from it, if you had read it when you were 18?

ELIF BATUMAN: What you said about heterosexuality reminded me of how poisonous I think the dynamics of heterosexuality are, and how I didn't really see it clearly in a catchy way until I read that book. Chris Kraus is like: "So I want to be feminine, I want to be dominated and fucked by this guy who's just a total jerk. Why can't that be an identity that I'm proud of, the way gay people are proud of their identities?" It's such a brilliant question.

I just wish I had read that sooner. I used to blame myself. I would be like: "Why do I choose these douche-bags and why do I want them to push me around?" And just to know that it's a combination of biology and statistics: you want to be pushed around because you're wired that way, and you want to be pushed around by some douchebag because most people are just douchebags, and you can't find anyone better. I was ashamed of it for years, for my whole life, and then I would waste time with guys who weren't going to push me around.

I thought it was hilarious how she was just making fun of this guy for the whole time. The fact that he's such a douche could be hilarious, and she and her husband leaving twenty-minute-long messages on his answering machine is hilarious. It could be something playful.

———

Elizabeth's nine lives

DAYNA TORTORICI: Elizabeth, I fear that everything you've said about yourself so far has been slightly opaque. A reader who doesn't know you will have no idea what you do.

ELIZABETH GUMPORT: I don't know what I do.

DAYNA TORTORICI: That's not true.

ELIZABETH GUMPORT: Yes it is!

DAYNA TORTORICI: Is it?

ELIZABETH GUMPORT: Yeah! I have no idea what I do or want to do. I assume this will be another past life at some point.

AMANDA KATZ: What would someone else say you do? I mean, I don't really know you.

ELIZABETH GUMPORT: Right now I'm a grad student, which is a horrible thing to say about someone. But I feel like I'm waiting for a next life to start, in the sense that I don't have a set of things that I feel particularly inspired or activated by right now. It goes in cycles. That partially defines what I mean by "a life"—what is a past life, or what is a present life. So I'm waiting for the next life. Which is kind of a good feeling, but it comes after a bad feeling, the bad feeling of exhausting everything that you do have. Which is how I feel every time I read Henry James. Every time I read Henry James I feel like I'm never going to read anything that good again, my life might as well just end now.

ELIF BATUMAN: I feel like that too, with the three that I like.

ELIZABETH GUMPORT: After *The Wings of the Dove* and *The Golden Bowl* I was just devastated.

ELIF BATUMAN: Also *Portrait of a Lady*.

ELIZABETH GUMPORT: And *The Ambassadors*, sort of.

ELIF BATUMAN: Yes, sort of.

ASTRA TAYLOR: See, I get to read all of this.

ELIZABETH GUMPORT: (*Shouting*) I know! You get to read them! Your whole life is ahead of you!

Those books don't make me want to write. Those books make me feel completely devastated. But so grateful, too. Even though I haven't read them recently, that's kind of how I feel right now: just waiting to feel like I could do something again. I'm sure that wasn't helpful for anyone who doesn't know me.

Advice

ASTRA TAYLOR: The best advice I ever got was from Rebecca Solnit, maybe twelve years ago. She told me to live below my means. Just no matter how low your means are, live below them.

ELIF BATUMAN: Is that the same as saying save money?

ASTRA TAYLOR: No.

ELIF BATUMAN: What's the difference?

ASTRA TAYLOR: Well, saving money means adding another aspect of responsibility, right? Then you'd actually have to be overachieving, you'd have to be making more money than you live on. Living below your means is just not going into debt, for example. Not spending all your money. I think the subtext of it was: embrace bohemia.

ELIF BATUMAN: It's the opposite of save money. Save money is all, "Be all right wing."

ASTRA TAYLOR: I think that was it. It pointed toward an intellectually engaged life that was in bohemia and not in academia.

DAYNA TORTORICI: The best advice I've ever gotten was actually from you, Astra. Twice.

ASTRA TAYLOR: Really? Double? Twice?

DAYNA TORTORICI: The first time was when I was taking time off from school. I didn't want to go back, and you said, "Go back, why not, but read history. Learn economics. Do things you'll never want to do on your own."

ASTRA TAYLOR: Yes. Why did I study calculus? I should have studied statistics. Then I could go and argue with people.

DAYNA TORTORICI: The other bit of advice was when I was about to start a really shitty job at a shitty corporation. You said, "It's OK to quit. A mind is a terrible thing to waste." And I did quit, on my first day.

ASTRA TAYLOR: But it's not like you quit everything. You just quit things that suck.

NAMARA SMITH: That was the best advice I ever got, too. "You can quit your bad job." Also, if you're interviewing for a job, or looking for something that you want to do, it's not just about them liking you, it's about you liking them. After college I was always getting depressed because I would go into interviews and people just wouldn't like me. I'd be like, "Why? I tried to do everything right, what's wrong?" But I learned that maybe if they don't choose you it's actually a good thing for you, too. Whenever my parents or older friends said this to me, I'd get really mad. I'd be like, "You don't understand. You don't understand the economic situation, you don't understand what I want." It took me a long time to realize that it was really true. Why should you try to make yourself fit into some job that you don't even like? Maybe they're recognizing something about you that you don't recognize, and that's actually a good thing.

ELIF BATUMAN: I can only think of super specific advice I've gotten. I got good clothes advice. I had to learn at a very late age about buying clothes because they suit your body, as opposed to how they look.

ASTRA TAYLOR: I had to be taught that too late in life.

AMANDA KATZ: This is fashion advice!

ELIF BATUMAN: Yeah, fashion advice.

NAMARA SMITH: Fashion advice has a lot of metaphorical extension.

ELIF BATUMAN: It ties into the whole subject. I feel like I've learned very late how important (*laughing*) human subjectivity is. How different other people's perception of you is from your perception of yourself, and how different your perception of other people is from their perception of themselves. Which is something that every writer really needs to learn much sooner rather than later, and I came to it late, but, you know, better late than never.

I have this idea that I don't look like anything—everyone else looks very specific and I just kind of look like whatever. It's not true. It's not true! There's a specific way that you look, and your eyes are a particular color, and your legs are some weird way or whatever, and you have to work with that. My feet are a different size than I thought they were for years, which taught me a lot about self-deception. A friend of mine was saying the other day, "I've just realized at age 32 that I've always been getting my shoes the wrong size." I was like, "How could you not tell?" and he said, "Well, I just thought it was normal for my shoes to be slightly uncomfortable." I've had that with so many things. I just thought that that's what sweaters were—like, they just make you look kind of bad. But that's not true.

ASTRA TAYLOR: You probably had a certain freedom, though, having this perspective.

ELIF BATUMAN: I did, I did. I know. I wasn't the sober, drab person you see before you today.

The other thing is, just as I think I have no appearance, I think I have no personality—I think that I'm totally malleable. Whatever I say is just an expression of what I feel like at a particular moment, whereas when other people say things it's a representation of some deeply held belief essential to their identity, a belief they've had for a really long time and feel really confident and stable about. Especially when I was younger, writing about people who were older than me, I would make them sound puppet-like. Sometimes they would be irritated, and I wouldn't understand why. I mean my feeling was, "But you actually said that."

In my book I had a scene in a creative writing workshop where the instructor, Rob Cohen, goes around the table and goes, "You're gonna die, you're gonna die, you're gonna die," and that's the only time he appears in the whole book. And he wasn't thrilled about it. He was like, "When I was saying that, I thought I was being funny, but in this scene I sound kind of gloomy. I thought I was going to come back later in the story and say something a little cooler, but I didn't come back. I just said this gloomy thing and then left." I love Rob Cohen, and I loved that he said we were all going to die, so I felt terrible about that. We actually had this exchange when "Babel in California" came out, eight years ago.* And a friend of mine just went and saw Rob, he's at Middlebury now, and he said, "Tell Elif I have great news. That thing about how we're all going to die? It turns out that, with the right Mediterranean diet, we can avoid that whole thing." Which is hilarious, but also, you know—I thought, "Oh, he still remembers that."

I had similar trouble doing profile journalism. Sometimes your idea of a person just doesn't coincide at all with their idea of themselves. I didn't realize what a violent thing it is to do to someone. I didn't realize how angry people can be. In my life, the times when people have been the most angry, like, the most ballistic, out of control batshit angry at me, in professional and personal life, was when I was somehow the instrument of their self-image being changed in some way. So just to realize what a potent and dangerous thing that is—it's something you can learn from fashion advice.

ASTRA TAYLOR: One lesson I can share from life is that you should let certain things go unattended—prioritize and let yourself be, for example, messy. The work is more important than the dirty dishes. The work is

---

* See "Babel in California" by Elif Batuman in *n+1* Issue Two, "Happiness."

more important than paying the bills on time. And I feel like that was something in my early twenties that I consciously cultivated in myself. I was very struck by my partner, who's very creative and everything could go to hell if he's in the zone. I would be trotting around, older sister that I am, responsible, nurturer, cleaning up or taking care of things, and then I sort of had this epiphany: Why the resentment? Why should I act like that? And now I'm probably the bigger slob of the pair.

ELIF BATUMAN: Well played.

ASTRA TAYLOR: Thank you. He does the dishes every night. And to just self-consciously get out of that habit of attending to the environment when ultimately it doesn't fucking matter, it's my environment and if there are other things I want to prioritize, I should stop procrastinating and do my work. That was a big shift. I really practiced being a slob.

ELIF BATUMAN: My shorthand for that is Being a Dude. It's been hard for me, and immensely rewarding whenever I can make myself do it.

DAYNA TORTORICI: Be a dude?

ELIF BATUMAN: Yeah. Don't answer your emails on time if you don't feel like writing to the person . . .

ELIZABETH GUMPORT: I feel like I've had to fight in the other direction, 'cause I've never taken care of anything. And if I do that to the extreme, where I'm in a position where there's no one to do it, I'll just die! I won't even eat! I won't do anything.

DAYNA TORTORICI: Are you saying you need a wife?

ELIF BATUMAN: That's exactly what I was thinking.

ELIZABETH GUMPORT: Yeah, actually. Yeah.

AMANDA KATZ: I have a problem with this narrative, though. When women say they need a wife, it's just kind of . . . ehh. I want the Jacques Demy/Agnès Varda model, where everyone gets to make movies; I'm discontent with the idea that someone's going to be the wife. I want partnerships where no one is the caretaker and the picker-up-after. I think that, if you're the kind of person who drinks coffee but doesn't know how to make it, you probably need to be pushed toward being a little more responsible. But for a lot of people, for a lot of women, I do think it is learning to be a bit more like a dude, and learning to put yourself out there and assume that your stuff is good, and let other things slide.

I deal with this as an editor and as a writer all the time. As an editor I spend lots of time being like: Women, send me your stuff, even if you think it's not done, and even if you think it's not perfect. Trust me, guys will send me things that are crap—they will send me lots and lots of crap, and eventually one of those pieces of crap will get chosen to be published or be produced or whatever. It's your duty as a feminist to be putting your stuff out there, and it's one of the only ways that you can remember to do it. But then I see myself as a writer being quite shy, waiting until people solicit things from me, even then maybe if something doesn't work out it's hard for me to resubmit. I totally play into it, too, on the other side. It's a challenge, it's a constant effort.

ASTRA TAYLOR: This relates to something Elif said at the beginning, about how as an aspiring writer she believed she should not read novels in order to be a real, creative genius. I love my influences, but I would advise people to be more like young Elif! Protect and cultivate and trust your untrammeled instincts a little bit, just for fun.

I think a lot of people, young women especially, have the opposite problem. They feel they need to know everything, to have read all the literature and gathered all the facts and figures and have the appropriate degrees and validations, before they can take a stab at creating art, or participating in the broader cultural conversation, or putting themselves forward for a job, or whatever. I'm thinking, for example, of my 21-year-old sister, who just told me that she only knows two girls in bands, and that they both graduated from music school, whereas every boy on the street fancies himself a musician though most can probably barely play power chords. I was really struck by this, that the only girls she knows in Portland who play music are highly credentialed, when you truly do not need to know much of anything to make sounds that someone, somewhere, may like listening to.

What would Henry James do?

DAYNA TORTORICI: What books changed your life, in discrete and palpable ways?

ASTRA TAYLOR: Reading *Wanderlust* by Rebecca Solnit definitely planted the seed that became my second film, *Examined Life*. There was something about that connection she drew between thinking, walking, politics, and inhabiting the world as physical space that really got my imagination going.

ELIF BATUMAN: All of my anxieties were informed by *The Portrait of a Lady*. I read it when I was 20, on a night bus in Turkey. I was so struck by the plot—by the way Ralph gives Isabel all that money so she can live an interesting life and be an edifying spectacle to him in his infirmity. If she got rich at the end, that would be a happy ending—but at the beginning, it creates the whole problem of the book. I was also really influenced by a passage where Isabel is wondering whether she'll be misunderstood—and then the narrator says, "she always remembered that one should never regret a generous error and that if Madame Merle had not the merits she attributed to her, so much the worse for Madame Merle." For a long time, whenever I was undecided about anything, I would on principle make the more extravagant, less conservative choice.

AMANDA KATZ: It's certainly not the only answer in this category for me, but *Autobiography of Red* by Anne Carson. It was a book that made me feel like you can put a lot of different types of things into one book—that a book can be that expansive.

ELIF BATUMAN: I got that from Marina Tsvetaeva's *My Pushkin*, too. She's a poet and she's writing about her encounters with Pushkin and how those encounters are themselves a story. It wasn't criticism, but it was critical, and it turned these texts into these living things that were in her life like people. And it was short. It felt manageable. It made writing seem doable.

NAMARA SMITH: In school, the two most important books I read were *War and Peace* and *The Brothers Karamazov*. I had a Henry James moment two years ago that was really important for me, when I read *The Ambassadors*. But then, really, in the last three or four years, it's just been a lot of things by people at *n+1*. Those are the things that I read. It's a community of people that's real in the world right now.

ELIZABETH GUMPORT: I was trying to think of something besides Henry James for my answer to what changed your life. There was a period—I guess after I read *The Wings of the Dove*, but also *The Golden Bowl* and *The Ambassadors*—when I would just ask myself and other people constantly: "What would Henry James do?" Answering that changed my life in concrete, specific ways.

DAYNA TORTORICI: Can you tell a story about one of those times?

ELIZABETH GUMPORT: I can't tell any of the stories.

ELIF BATUMAN: Like, what would he do as a historical figure?

ELIZABETH GUMPORT: No, because he wouldn't do anything. But what would he have happen, or want you to do.

DAYNA TORTORICI: So it's like if you were Henry James's heroine, and he was calling the shots in your life, what he would want you to do.

ELIZABETH GUMPORT: Yes, and I made all his mistakes. I did. So that changed my life.

AMANDA KATZ: It could have been a worse person. It could have been Jacqueline Susann.

ELIZABETH GUMPORT: Oh, he was the perfect person.

ELIF BATUMAN: It could have been Jack London.

DAYNA TORTORICI: What would Jack London do? Christ. You'd be dead.

ELIZABETH GUMPORT: Jacqueline Susann would have involved a lot more pills, probably. Yes, if it was anyone, I'm glad it was Henry James.

——

Last words

DAYNA TORTORICI: Any final advice?

ELIF BATUMAN: (*Bully voice*) Stay in school.

AMANDA KATZ: Don't make the same mistakes I did!

ELIZABETH GUMPORT: And never fuck up.

ELIF BATUMAN: My aunt used to give that advice. She would whisper, "I'm going to give you this piece of really good advice . . ." And I'd say, "What?" Then she'd be like, "Don't fuck up!!" She'd do it at the end of every phone conversation. She's a tiny Turkish lady. It was really cute. +

BOOKS THAT CHANGED MY LIFE

Group one

Kristin Dombek

Richard Brautigan, *In Watermelon Sugar*

Bertolt Brecht, *Brecht on Theatre*

J. M. Coetzee, *The Lives of Animals*

Jacques Derrida, *The Gift of Death*

Joan Didion, *Slouching Towards Bethlehem*

W. E. B. DuBois, *Black Reconstruction in America*

René Girard, *Violence and the Sacred*

William Faulkner, *Absalom, Absalom!*

David Harvey, *Justice, Nature, and the Geography of Difference*

Cormac McCarthy, *Blood Meridian*

Adrienne Rich, *The Fact of a Doorframe*

David Foster Wallace, *A Supposedly Fun Thing I'll Never Do Again*

Sara Marcus

(Books and music, in my teens and early twenties)

Bikini Kill, Self-titled EP

Judith Butler, "Imitation and Gender Insubordination"

John Cage, *A Year from Monday: New Lectures and Writings*

The Ex and Tom Cora, *And the Weathermen Shrug Their Shoulders*

Marilyn French, *The Women's Room*

Susie Ibarra, Live at Tonic 1999-2002

Meridel Le Sueur, *Salute to Spring*

New Masses, 1931–34

Grace Paley, *Later the Same Day*

Adrienne Rich, *The Fact of a Doorframe*

Team Dresch, *Captain My Captain*

David S. Ware, *Go See the World*

Dawn Lundy Martin

Judith Butler, *Gender Trouble*

J. M. Coetzee, *Disgrace*

Toi Derricotte, *The Black Notebooks*

Paul Lawrence Dunbar, *Poems of Cabin and Field*

Michel Foucault, *Discipline and Punish*

Susan Howe, *My Emily Dickinson*

Erica Jong, *Fear of Flying*

Adrienne Kennedy, *Funnyhouse of a Negro*

Audre Lorde, *Zami: A New Spelling of My Name—A Biomythography*

Myung Mi Kim, *Under Flag*

Adrian Piper, *Out of Order, Out of Sight, Vol. 1: Selected Writings in
    Meta Art 1968–1992*

Marcel Proust, *In Search of Lost Time*

Anne Sexton, *The Complete Poems*

Sarah Resnick

James Agee and Walker Evans, *Let Us Now Praise Famous Men*

Michelle Alexander, *The New Jim Crow*

Johanna Brenner, *Women and the Politics of Class*

Lydia Davis, *Almost No Memory*

Adrian Nicole LeBlanc, *Random Family*

Helen Levitt and James Agee, *A Way of Seeing*

Grace Paley, *Enormous Changes at the Last Minute*

Lynne Tillman, *American Genius*

Kathi Weeks, *The Problem with Work*

Dayna Tortorici

Roland Barthes, *Camera Lucida*; *The Pleasure of the Text*; *S/Z*

George Eliot, *Middlemarch*; *The Mill on the Floss*; "Silly Novels by Lady Novelists"

William Faulkner, *Absalom, Absalom!*

Shoshana Felman, ed. *Literature and Psychoanalysis*

Shulamith Firestone, *The Dialectic of Sex*

Michel Foucault, *The Birth of Biopolitics*

Sigmund Freud, *Three Essays on the Theory of Sexuality*

Elizabeth Hardwick, *Seduction and Betrayal*

Albert O. Hirschman, *The Passions and the Interests*

John Milton, *The Complete Works of John Milton*

Ovid, *The Metamorphoses*, trans. Allen Mandelbaum

Virginia Woolf, *The Common Reader*; *To the Lighthouse*

Group two

Carla Blumenkranz

Hannah Arendt, *Eichmann in Jerusalem*

Anton Chekhov, *Selected Stories of Anton Chekov,* trans. Richard
Pevear and Larissa Volokhonsky

Grace Paley, *Enormous Changes at the Last Minute*

Leo Tolstoy, *Anna Karenina*

Edith Wharton, *The Age of Innocence*

Virginia Woolf, *To the Lighthouse*

Emily Gould

Romy Ashby, *The Cutmouth Lady*

Colette, *Claudine at School*

Cookie Mueller, *Walking Through Clear Water in a Pool Painted Black*

Phoebe Gloeckner, *Diary of a Teenage Girl*

Chris Kraus, *I Love Dick*

Eileen Myles, *Chelsea Girls*

Philip Roth, *The Ghost Writer*

Sarah Schulman, *Gentrification of the Mind*

Ellen Willis, *No More Nice Girls*

Emily Witt

Simone de Beauvoir, *The Prime of Life*

Joan Didion, *Slouching Towards Bethlehem; The White Album*

Michel Foucault, *The History of Sexuality, Vol. 1; The Order of Things*

Doris Lessing, *The Golden Notebook*

Claude Lévi-Strauss, *Tristes Tropiques*

Thomas Pynchon, *Gravity's Rainbow*

David Foster Wallace, *A Supposedly Fun Thing I'll Never Do Again*;
　　Infinite Jest

Tom Wolfe, ed. *The New Journalism*

Group three

Elif Batuman

Isaac Babel, *Collected Stories*; *1920 Diary*

Miguel de Cervantes, *Don Quixote*

Arthur Conan Doyle, *Sherlock Holmes* series

Epictetus, *Discourses and Selected Writings*

Henry James, *Portrait of a Lady*

Fredric Jameson, *Marxism and Form*

Vladimir Nabokov, *Pale Fire*

Marcel Proust, *In Search of Lost Time*

Alexander Pushkin, *Eugene Onegin*

Viktor Shklovsky, *Zoo, or Letters Not About Love*

Leo Tolstoy, *Anna Karenina*

P. G. Wodehouse, Jeeves and Wooster series

Elizabeth Gumport

Martin Buber, *I and Thou*

Stanley Cavell, *Pursuits of Happiness*

Ralph Waldo Emerson, *Essays and Lectures*

Friedrich Engels, *The Origin of the Family, Private Property and the State*

Shulamith Firestone, *The Dialectic of Sex*

Michel Foucault, *Discipline and Punish*

Vivian Gornick, *The Solitude of Self*

Donna Haraway, *Simians, Cyborgs, and Women*

Elizabeth Hardwick, *Seduction and Betrayal*

Laura Kaplan, *The Story of Jane: The Legendary Underground Feminist Abortion Service*

Henry James, *The Ambassadors*; *The Golden Bowl*; *The Wings of the Dove*

Chris Kraus, *I Love Dick*

Ellen Willis, *No More Nice Girls*

Amanda Katz

John Ashbery, *Self-Portrait in a Convex Mirror*

Roland Barthes, *The Pleasure of the Text*

Anne Carson, *Autobiography of Red*

Michael Chabon, *The Amazing Adventures of Kavalier and Klay*

Julio Cortázar, *Blow-Up*; *Hopscotch*

W. G. Sebald, *The Rings of Saturn*

Gertrude Stein, *The Autobiography of Alice B. Toklas*; *Tender Buttons*

Virginia Woolf, *The Waves*

Namara Smith

Hannah Arendt, *The Human Condition*

Jane Austen, *Emma*

Fyodor Dostoevsky, *The Brothers Karamazov*

Euclid, *Elements*

Henry James, *The Ambassadors*

D. H. Lawrence, *Women in Love*

V. S. Naipaul, *The Enigma of Arrival*

Plato, *Theaetetus*

Leo Tolstoy, *War and Peace*

Edith Wharton, *House of Mirth*

Astra Taylor

Gilles Deleuze and Félix Guattari, *A Thousand Plateaus*

Barbara Ehrenreich, *Fear of Falling*

Michel Foucault, *Madness and Civilization*

Lewis Hyde, *The Gift*

James Joyce, *Ulysses*

Doris Lessing, *The Golden Notebook*

Karl Marx, *Capital*

Rebecca Solnit, *Wanderlust*

Ellen Willis, *No More Nice Girls*

WORKS MENTIONED

Agee, James and Walker Evans. *Let Us Now Praise Famous Men* (1941); James Agee and Helen Levitt. *A Way of Seeing* (1989).

Alexander, Michelle. *The New Jim Crow* (2010).

Arendt, Hannah. *Eichmann in Jerusalem* (1963); *The Human Condition* (1958).

Ashbery, John. *Self-Portrait in a Convex Mirror* (1975).

Ashby, Romy. *The Cutmouth Lady* (1995).

Austen, Jane. *Emma* (1815).

Babel, Isaac. *Collected Stories*; *1920 Diary* (1920).

Barthes, Roland. *Camera Lucida* (1980); *The Pleasure of the Text* (1973); *S/Z* (1970).

Batuman, Elif. *The Possessed* (2010).

Beckett, Samuel. *Molloy, Malone Dies, The Unnamable: A Trilogy* (1958).

Benjamin, Walter. "Unpacking My Library," in *Illuminations* (1955).

Brautigan, Richard. *In Watermelon Sugar* (1968).

Brecht, Bertolt. *Brecht on Theatre* (1918–1956).

Brenner, Johanna. *Women and the Politics of Class* (2000).

Buber, Martin. *I and Thou* (1923).

Bukowski, Charles. *Post Office* (1971).

Butler, Judith. "Imitation and Gender Insubordination," in *Gender Trouble* (1990).

Cage, John. *A Year from Monday: New Lectures and Writings* (1961–1967).

Carson, Anne. *Autobiography of Red* (1998).

Cavell, Stanley. *Pursuits of Happiness* (1981).

Chabon, Michael. *The Amazing Adventures of Kavalier and Klay* (2000).

Chekhov, Anton. *Selected Stories of Anton Chekhov*. Trans., Richard Pevear and Larissa Volokhonsky (2009).

Coetzee, J. M. *Disgrace* (1999); *The Lives of Animals* (1999).

Colette. *Claudine at School* (1900).

Cortázar, Julio. *Blow-Up* (1968); *Hopscotch* (1963).

Dalla Costa, Mariarosa and Selma James. "The Power of Women and the Subversion of the Community" (1975).

Davis, Lydia. *Almost No Memory* (1997).

de Beauvoir, Simone. *The Prime of Life* (1960).

de Cervantes, Miguel. *Don Quixote* (1605).

Deleuze, Gilles and Félix Guattari. *A Thousand Plateaus* (1980).

Derricotte, Toi. *The Black Notebooks* (1997).

Derrida, Jacques. *The Animal That Therefore I Am* (2008).

Dickens, Charles. *Bleak House* (1853).

Didion, Joan. *Slouching Towards Bethlehem* (1968); *The White Album* (1979).

Dillard, Annie. *Teaching a Stone to Talk* (1982).

Dostoevsky, Fyodor. *The Brothers Karamazov* (1880).

Doyle, Arthur Conan. *Sherlock Holmes* series (1887–1927).

Works Mentioned

DuBois, W. E. B. *Black Reconstruction in America* (1935).

Dunbar, Paul Lawrence. *Poems of Cabin and Field* (1899).

Echols, Alice. *Daring to Be Bad* (1989).

Ehrenreich, Barbara. *Fear of Falling* (1989).

Eisenstein, Sergei. Dir., *Strike* (1924); *Battleship Potemkin* (1925).

Eliot, George. *Middlemarch* (1874); *The Mill on the Floss* (1860); "Silly Novels by Lady Novelists" (1856).

Ellison, Ralph. *Invisible Man* (1952).

Emerson, Ralph Waldo. *Essays and Lectures* (1836–1870).

Engels, Friedrich. *The Origin of the Family, Private Property and the State* (1884).

Epictetus. *Discourses and Selected Writings* (c. 108 AD).

Euclid. *Elements* (c. 300 BCE).

The Ex and Tom Cora. *And the Weathermen Shrug Their Shoulders* (1993).

Faulkner, William. *Absalom, Absalom!* (1936).

Federici, Silvia. *Revolution at Point Zero* (2012).

Feinberg, Leslie. *Stone Butch Blues* (1993).

Felman, Shoshana. Ed., *Literature and Psychoanalysis* (1977).

Fielding, Helen. *Bridget Jones' Diary* (1996).

Finnegan, William. *A Complicated War* (1992); *Cold New World* (1998); *Crossing the Line* (1986); "The Last Tour," the *New Yorker* (September 29, 2008).

Firestone, Shulamith. "Down with Childhood," in *The Dialectic of Sex* (1970); Ed., *Notes from the Second Year* (1970).

Forster, E. M. *Howard's End* (1910).

Foucault, Michel. *The Birth of Biopolitics* (1970–1984); *Discipline and Punish* (1975); *The History of Sexuality, Vol. 1* (1976); *Madness and Civilization* (1964); *The Order of Things* (1966).

French, Marilyn. *The Women's Room* (1977).

Freud, Sigmund. *Three Essays on the Theory of Sexuality* (1905).

Frye, Northrop. *Anatomy of Criticism* (1957).

Girard, René. *Violence and the Sacred* (1972).

Gloeckner, Phoebe. *Diary of a Teenage Girl* (2002).

Gornick, Vivian. *The Solitude of Self* (2006).

Griffith, D. W. Dir., *The Birth of a Nation* (1915).

Haraway, Donna. *Simians, Cyborgs, and Women: The Reinvention of Nature* (1991).

Hardwick, Elizabeth. *Seduction and Betrayal* (1974).

Harvey, David. *Justice, Nature, and the Geography of Difference* (1996).

Hernandez, Gilbert and Jamie. *Love and Rockets* (1982–1996).

Hirschman, Albert O. *The Passions and the Interests* (1977).

Holleran, Andrew. *Chronicle of a Plague, Revisited* (2008).

Howe, Susan. *My Emily Dickinson* (1985).

Hyde, Lewis. *The Gift* (1983).

James, Henry. *The Ambassadors* (1903); *The Golden Bowl* (1904); *The Portrait of a Lady* (1881); *The Wings of the Dove* (1902).

Jameson, Fredric. *Marxism and Form* (1972).

Jong, Erica. *Fear of Flying* (1973).

Joyce, James. *Ulysses* (1922).

Kaplan, Laura. *The Story of Jane: The Legendary Underground Feminist Abortion Service* (1997).

Kapuściński, Ryszard. *Another Day of Life* (1976).

Kennedy, Adrienne. *Funnyhouse of a Negro* (1969).

Kerouac, Jack. *On the Road* (1957).

Kim, Myung Mi. *Under Flag* (1991).

King, Stephen. *Carrie* (1974).

Klein, Naomi. *No Logo* (1999).

Kraus, Chris. *I Love Dick* (1997).

Lawrence, D. H. *Women in Love* (1920).

Le Sueur, Meridel. *Salute to Spring* (1940).

LeBlanc, Adrian Nicole. *Random Family* (2003).

Lee, Harper. *To Kill a Mockingbird* (1960).

Lessing, Doris. *The Golden Notebook* (1962).

Lethem, Jonathan. *The Fortress of Solitude* (2003).

Lévi-Strauss, Claude. *Tristes Tropiques* (1955).

Lispector, Clarice. *The Passion According to G. H.* (1964).

Lorde, Audre. *Zami: A New Spelling of My Name: A Biomythography* (1982).

Lumière, Auguste and Louis. Dir., short films in *Landmarks of Early Film, Vol. 1, 1902* (1997).

Malcolm, Janet. *The Journalist and the Murderer* (1990); *The Silent Woman* (1994).

Mallarmé, Stéphane. "A Tomb for Anatole" (1961).

Marx, Karl. *Capital, Vol.1* (1867).

McCarthy, Cormac. *Blood Meridian* (1985).

Melville, Herman. *Moby-Dick* (1851).

Miller, Henry. *Nexus* (1959); *Plexus* (1953); *Sexus* (1949).

Milton, John. *The Complete Works of John Milton* (1680).

Mueller, Cookie. *Walking Through Clear Water In A Pool Painted Black* (1990).

Move Into the Villa Villakula. Various artists. CD (1994).

Mulvey, Laura. "Visual Pleasure and Narrative Cinema" in *Screen* 16.3, Autumn 1975. pp. 6–18 (1975).

Myles, Eileen. *Chelsea Girls* (1994).

Nabokov, Vladimir. *Pale Fire* (1962).

Naipaul, V. S. *The Enigma of Arrival* (1987).

Niffenegger, Audrey. *The Time Traveler's Wife* (2003).

Ovid. *The Metamorphoses*. Trans., Allen Mandelbaum (1995).

Paley, Grace. *Enormous Changes at the Last Minute* (1974); *Later the Same Day* (1985).

Piper, Adrian. *Out of Order, Out of Sight, Vol. 1: Selected Writings in Meta Art 1968–1992* (1996); "Self-Portrait as a Nice White Lady" (1995); "Self-Portrait Exaggerating My Negroid Features" (1981).

Plath, Sylvia. *The Bell Jar* (1963).

Plato. *Theaetetus* (c. 369 BCE).

Proust, Marcel. *In Search of Lost Time* (1913).

Pushkin, Alexander. *Eugene Onegin* (1825).

Pynchon, Thomas. *The Crying of Lot 49* (1966); *Gravity's Rainbow* (1973).

Ramas, Maria and Johanna Brenner. "Rethinking Women's Oppression." *New Left Review*, Vol. I No. 144, March–April 1984. *See* Brenner, Johanna.

Réage, Pauline. *The Story of O* (1954).

Rich, Adrienne. *The Fact of a Doorframe* (1984).

Roth, Philip. *American Pastoral* (1997); *The Counterlife* (1986); *The Ghost Writer* (1979); *The Human Stain* (2000); *Goodbye Columbus* (1959); *Portnoy's Complaint* (1969).

Salinger, J. D. *The Catcher in the Rye* (1951).

Schulman, Sarah. *The Gentrification of the Mind* (2012).

Sebald, W. G. *The Rings of Saturn* (1995).

Sexton, Anne. *The Complete Poems* (1999); *Transformations* (1971).

Shakur, Assata. *Assata: An Autobiography* (1987).

Shklovsky, Viktor. *Zoo, or Letters Not About Love* (1923).

Shteyngart, Gary. *Super Sad True Love Story* (2010).

Works Mentioned

Singer, Isaac Bashevis. *Enemies, A Love Story* (1966).

Smith, Zadie. *NW* (2012).

Solnit, Rebecca. *Wanderlust* (2000).

Snow, Michael. Dir., *Wavelength* (1967).

Spanbauer, Tom. *In the City of Shy Hunters* (2001).

Stein, Gertrude. *The Autobiography of Alice B. Toklas* (1933); *Tender Buttons* (1914).

Stone, Oliver. Dir., *Natural Born Killers* (1994).

Taylor, Astra. Dir., *Examined Life* (2008).

Tillman, Lynne. *American Genius: A Comedy* (2006).

Tolstoy, Leo. *Anna Karenina* (1877); *War and Peace* (1869).

Tsvetaeva, Marina. *My Pushkin* (1999).

Walker, Alice. *The Color Purple* (1982).

Wallace, David Foster. *Infinite Jest.* (1996); *A Supposedly Fun Thing I'll Never Do Again* (1997).

Waugh, Evelyn. *Decline and Fall* (1928).

Weeks, Kathi. *The Problem with Work* (2011).

Wharton, Edith. *The Age of Innocence* (1920); *The House of Mirth* (1905).

Willis, Ellen. *No More Nice Girls* (1992).

Wodehouse, P. G. Jeeves and Wooster series (1918–1974).

Wolfe, Cary. *Zoontologies* (2003).

Wolfe, Tom. Ed., *The New Journalism* (1973).

Woolf, Virginia. *Between the Acts* (1941); *The Common Reader* (1925); *Mrs Dalloway* (1925); *A Room of One's Own* (1929); *To the Lighthouse* (1927); *The Waves* (1931).

X, Malcolm and Alex Haley, *The Autobiography of Malcolm X* (1965).